# US BOMBERS
## OF WORLD WAR TWO

The breathtaking north-
western lakes of Washington
state, usually shrouded by
murk, pass beneath chin
turret-equipped B-17G
Fortress 42-97246 on an
early test flight. By the
middle of the war, Fortresses
were no longer being
camouflaged and more than
7,000 of the B-17G model
were delivered in natural
metal finish. (Boeing)

# US BOMBERS
## OF WORLD WAR TWO

## - ROBERT F. DORR -

ARMS AND
ARMOUR

*For John Bull Sterling*

British Library Cataloguing in Publication Data:
Dorr, Robert F., *1939–*
US bombers of World War Two.
1. United States. Air Force. Bomber aeroplanes, 1928–1980
I. Title
623.74'63'0973

ISBN 0-85368-943-1

Designed and edited by DAG Publications Ltd.
Designed by David Gibbons; layout by Anthony A. Evans;
typeset by Typesetters (Birmingham) Ltd., Warley, West
Midlands; camerawork by M&E Reproductions, North
Fambridge, Essex; printed and bound in Great Britain by The
Bath Press, Avon.

**Acknowledgments:** Any errors in this volume are the sole responsibility of the author. The book would have been impossible, however, without the generosity of many who helped.

This work is dedicated to John Bull Stirling, who flew B-26 Marauders in the Pacific and was still fighting for freedom two wars later.

Assistance was provided by the Department of Defense; I am especially grateful to Dan Howard, Bob Bockman and Ken Carter in the Pentagon.

I also wish to thank David A. Anderton, Kearney Bothwell, Vincent J. DiMattina Jr., Richard Foster, Harry Gann, Roland P. Gill, David R. McLaren, Donald S. McGarry, R. J. Mills Jr., Dave Ostrowski, Lt Cdr Dave Parsons, Marilyn Phipps, Norman Polmar, the gang at Roy's, Eric Simonsen, Jim Sullivan, Gordon Swanborough, Norman Taylor, Chris Westhorp and Douglas A. Zalud.

The views expressed in this book are mine and do not necessarily reflect those of the Department of State or of the United States Air Force.

Robert F. Dorr

# Contents

# Introduction

The idea of conducting warfare by air via the saturation bombing of civilian targets was first developed in World War One but at that stage could only have limited effect owing to the nature of primitive aviation technology. During the inter-war years, and the growth in aerial power and armament, the concept was again put into practice – this time with devastating effects – in the Spanish Civil War. The incendiaries and blitz bombing of Spain's Republican-held cities were a laboratory for the air forces of Germany and Italy; their expertise would not be wasted.

By 1940 Britain was engaged in a life and death struggle with the Luftwaffe in the skies over England. Having secured air superiority, Britain returned the blitz in kind: the German home front now suffered as they had made others suffer. It was not, however, only the Royal Air Force that took the war to the enemy, but also the might of a freshly unleashed latent power – the United States.

Having felt the effects of aerial bombardment and its accompanying destruction of infrastructure, war-making capacity and potential to undermine morale, the Allies felt that a concerted campaign of aerial bombing would complement the war on land and serve to squeeze Germany into submission while simultaneously encouraging morale on the home front and in the services. Only with the entry of the United States into the war did the capacity to do this become a reality. While Britain needed fighter aircraft and engaged in air support of the land war, home defence and shipping lane protection, the United States stepped up its programme of constructing powerful purpose-built aircraft solely for offensive bombing missions. The American aviation industry excelled in its task, free from the threat of air attack itself and with a vast industrial capacity to harness. Designs were produced and then tested with the British; once proved, and with the US now drawn into the conflict, immense production lines churned out thousands of the machines which would reduce Germany to rubble.

What was little more than an idea forty years previously had become an impressive and terrifying reality. Warfare would never be the same again.

Vapour trails, churning engines, open bomb bay doors. The Boeing B-17 Flying Fortress originally had no clear mission except to protect ocean-locked American shores from an enemy fleet. The US decision to mount a massive daylight bombing campaign over Hitler's 'Festung Europa' (Fortress Europe) gave a mission to the B-17 and made it perhaps the best-known US bomber of World War II. (Boeing)

# B-17 Flying Fortress

**T**he United States lost twelve thousand bombers in World War II – *big* bombers, that is. This figure, much overlooked, proclaims the simple truth that the men who fought the long-range air war in Flying Fortresses, Liberators and Superfortresses faced just as much risk and sacrifice as the infantrymen on the ground. And it does not even include those who fought in light and medium bombers – the Havocs, Bostons, Mitchells, Marauders.

Twelve thousand bombers, with a typical crew of ten men, four of them officers: that adds up to the male population of a major wartime city such as Bayonne, New Jersey. And the losses occurred in part, at least, because the United States chose daylight bombing. Daylight bombing in a B-17 which

carried ten men, as contrasted to the RAF's practice of night bombing in a Lancaster which did the same job with a crew of seven. Could not the Americans, renowned for devising machines to save labour, design a seven-man bomber? Did the United States – often criticized for its contempt of frugality and its tendency to waste – waste a generation of bomber crews?

Few now accept that the strategic bombing effort over the European continent achieved all that it was originally claimed to have achieved. Bombing was not as accurate as the top brass said it was. Bombing was not as effective as men like General Curtis E. LeMay insisted it was. Relentless pounding by the US Eighth and Fifteenth Air Forces did not cripple German industry, did not halt German fighter production, did not – until the final months – wipe away the enemy's fuel supply, and did not sap the will of the Third Reich to fight to the end.

Yet the bombing forced Nazi Germany to decentralize and disperse its fighter production, doing more harm to the Reich's aircraft industry than a thousand bombs exploding on factory buildings. The bombing forced Germany – and Japan – to shift resources which might otherwise have been used in the land and naval conflicts. And if the bombing did not quite cripple the Reich, it did inflict unacceptable losses.

In the Pacific, where experience from Europe was as valuable as any weapon, bombing eventually crippled a nation and in the end rendered unnecessary the planned amphibious invasion of the Japanese home islands. Twelve thousand aircraft is a monstrous loss. It is perhaps a quarter of all the US bombers manufactured during the war. But it was, in the end, a necessary price.

By the end of the war, vast armadas equipped primarily with the Boeing B-17 Flying Fortress ranged far and wide over Germany and occupied Europe, bombing railheads, factories and supply centres and bleeding off the fighter strength of the Luftwaffe in some of the biggest and most brutal air battles ever fought. On a typical mission, a B-17 could carry a modest bomb load to a combat radius of more than 800 miles, putting most of Europe within its reach from the British Isles. This was a towering achievement and it came only a few short years after the United States had had no real bomber force at all.

## Embryo Air Arm

In 1934, in an innocent era of peacetime, the US Army Air Corps had a few Martin B-10 monoplane bombers, not capable of carrying very much or of

B-17F overall dimensions and areas.

It took plenty of people to put a B-17 Fortress into the air and to keep it there. When a Fortress was lost with a full ten-man crew, the loss was felt throughout a squadron. 'Hells Angels', a B-17E in England, poses with the full ground and flight crews involved in keeping the aircraft in combat. (Boeing)

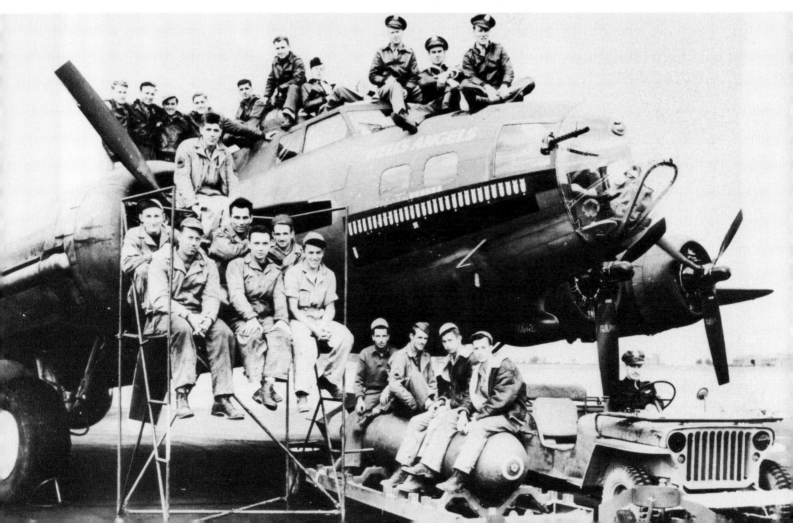

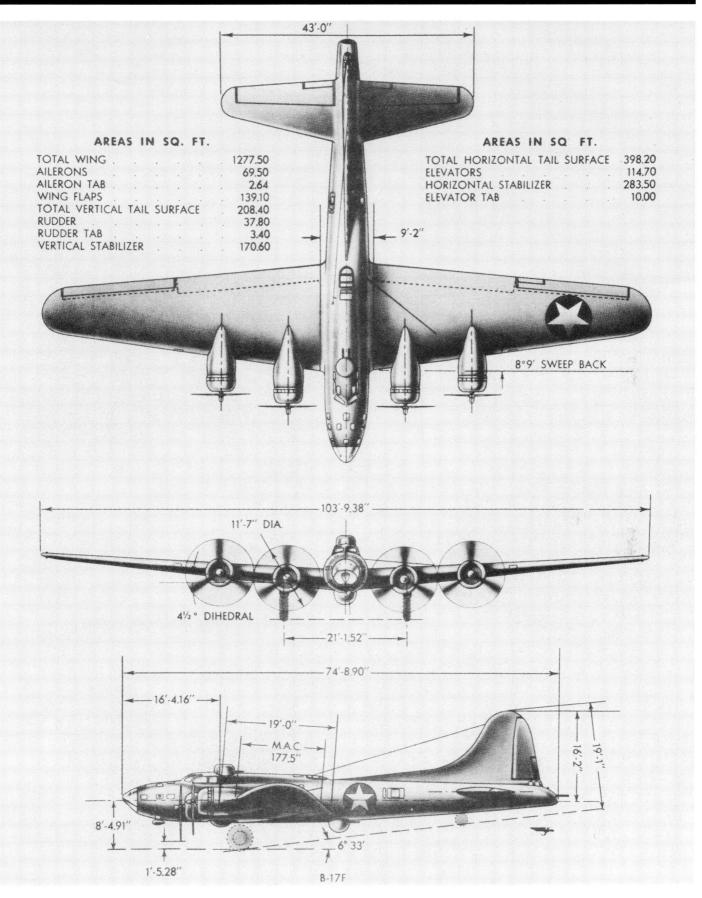

43'-0"

## AREAS IN SQ. FT.

| | |
|---|---|
| TOTAL WING | 1277.50 |
| AILERONS | 69.50 |
| AILERON TAB | 2.64 |
| WING FLAPS | 139.10 |
| TOTAL VERTICAL TAIL SURFACE | 208.40 |
| RUDDER | 37.80 |
| RUDDER TAB | 3.40 |
| VERTICAL STABILIZER | 170.60 |

## AREAS IN SQ. FT.

| | |
|---|---|
| TOTAL HORIZONTAL TAIL SURFACE | 398.20 |
| ELEVATORS | 114.70 |
| HORIZONTAL STABILIZER | 283.50 |
| ELEVATOR TAB | 10.00 |

9'-2"

8°9' SWEEP BACK

103'-9.38"

11'-7" DIA.

4½° DIHEDRAL

21'-1.52"

74'-8.90"

16'-4.16"

19'-0"

M.A.C. 177.5"

19'-1"

16'-2"

8'-4.91"

6° 33'

1'-5.28"

B-17F

9

going very far. The officer responsible for deciding the composition of the nation's future bombing force was a lieutenant colonel. The most influential designer at the company then contemplating a new bomber, Boeing, was a scant twenty-four years old. It was not merely an era of innocence but one of Hard Times. In the throes of the Depression, protected by two oceans from the troubles of an outside world, the American people worried about survival of home and family, not about building a bomber force.

The Boeing company had achieved remarkable success during the Depression with its Monomail (Model 200), Model 247 airliner and B-9 bomber. The B-9 was an open-cockpit monoplane with two engines and was one of the fastest aircraft in its category, vulnerable to contemporary fighters only under tightly defined conditions. But as impressive as the B-9 may have been, Boeing engineers took a quantum leap forward in planning their response to the US Army Air Corps' requirement for a next-generation bomber. In 1934 the Army said it wanted a 'multi-engine' bomber and Boeing took this to mean not two engines but four.

Other Army requirements included a range of 1,000 miles and a bomb load of 4,000lb. Boeing

Once the 'arsenal of democracy' had its production lines running at full speed, bombers churned out of the factory faster than men could paint them. These are natural-metal B-17G Fortresses at Seattle. The only aircraft serial number readily visible is 43-37582 (second from right, upper row). Several others have yet to receive numbers or national insignia. (Boeing)

The aircraft which started it all was the Boeing company's private venture, the Model 299, which led to the B-17 Flying Fortress. The civil-registered (NX 13372) Model 299 did not survive for long, but its loss in an accident was not the result of any flaw in the design. (Boeing)

responded with the company Model 299, the design of which began on 18 June 1934, initially under project chief E. G. Embry. By September 1934 when the configuration of the Model 299 had been decided, Edward C. Wells succeeded to the role of chief engineer at the age of twenty-four.

Wells and his team must have seemed audacious – perhaps foolishly so – in moving ahead with a huge, nearly all-metal four-engined bomber to repel an enemy invasion fleet; the protection of American shores was, after all, the only purpose for which anyone could then imagine having a large bomber. Furthermore, the Boeing engineers seemed more than a little prone to exaggeration when they christened their new offspring 'Flying Fortress' (during the war when the USAAF gave official names to aircraft the B-17 was known simply as the Fortress). But metal was cut and the Model 299 prototype became a reality in a surprisingly short time.

Unpainted except for Air Corps rudder stripes, a company emblem on the tail, and the civil registration X13372, the silver Model 299 prototype was rolled out on 17 July 1935 and took to the air for the first time on 28 July 1935 with Boeing chief test pilot Leslie R. Tower at the controls.

The Model 299 was powered by four 750hp Pratt & Whitney R-1690-E Hornet engines and had a distinctive single-leg main landing gear. To anyone who asked, pilot Tower quickly made it known that this aircraft was the hottest thing in the skies. To prove the point, on 20 August 1935 Tower flew the bomber from Seattle to Wright Field near Dayton, Ohio, covering 2,100 miles at an average speed of 232mph and using only 63 per cent of the 3,000hp available. Army officers, including Lt-Col Robert G. Olds who had the task of developing future bomber strategy, were impressed.

Then . . . disaster. On 30 October 1935 with Major P. O. Hill as pilot on the first officially observed flight before USAAC evaluation officers, the Model 299

climbed out, stalled, dipped a wing at a precarious angle, and crashed. The ensuing fire consumed the aircraft. Pilot Hill – who had omitted to release an external lock on the elevators – died instantly. Les Tower, aboard as an observer, succumbed to his injuries a few days later.

Despite the loss of this impressive aircraft and the declaration of the lacklustre Douglas B-18 as winner in the official trials, the Air Corps had seen enough to believe in the potential of the Flying Fortress. On 17 January 1936 the service placed an order for thirteen machines, designated Y1B-17 (the 'Y1' prefix signifying that funding was separate from regular Air Corps appropriations). On 1 March 1937 the first operational four-engined bomber in American livery, Y1B-17 Flying Fortress 36-149, arrived at Langley Field near Hampton, Virginia, to join the 2nd Bombardment Group commanded by Olds.

The B-17, as it became known after service tests, differed from the Model 299 in having 930hp Wright R-1820-39 Cyclone engines and revised landing gear and armament. Externally the aircraft was little changed. Once the twelfth and final B-17 had been delivered on 5 August 1937 (the thirteenth went to Wright Field for tests while the fourteenth airframe, the Y1B-17A, was employed to evaluate turbo-superchargers), Olds and his crews set forth to do some remarkable pioneering work in bomber development. They demonstrated that four engines made it possible to achieve greater height over target. They devised heavy bombing techniques. In time, they logged 9,293 hours under a gruelling variety of flight and weather conditions without ever losing an aircraft.

On 12 May 1938 Lt Col Robert Olds despatched a mission which demonstrated that the Flying Fortress could perform the job everyone envisaged for it. After all, with the United States protected by vast oceans, the main task of a heavy bomber had to be the bombing of hostile navy fleets offshore – or so

The view from the waist-gunner's position. If it was another Fortress out there, like the B-17E visible in the background, it was a source of comfort. But gunners, who braved almost inhuman conditions and sub-zero cold, knew they might be looking at a Focke-Wulf or a Messerschmitt. On the B-17E model the arc of the machine-gun had severe limits and it was a real struggle to zero in on a Luftwaffe fighter. (USAF)

Vega-built B-17G Fortress 44-8485 of the 100th Bomb Group, in latter-day natural metal, is seen at Haguenaw Airfield, France, in autumn 1944. (via Norman Taylor)

The wartime censor who released this view of B-17E Flying Fortress 41-2567 with no clue as to its date or location managed, at least, to inform readers that the aircraft was flying at 18,000ft (5,486m) with its bay doors open after dropping bombs. The 'E' model lacked the chin turret found on later Fortresses but was at least armed with a tail gun. (USAF)

Characteristic early view of the Boeing Model 299 which became the B-17 Flying Fortress. (USAF)

This early view of one of the very first B-17 Flying Fortress bombers – as yet without tail gun or other turrets – was taken at Langley Field, Virginia, on 24 February 1938. (USAF)

everyone thought. (Everybody, that is, except certain US Navy admirals who thought differently and the general public which rarely thought about the matter at all). Three Fortresses of the 49th Bomb Group were sent to intercept the *Rex*, an Italian luxury liner making its way across the Atlantic nearly 800 miles (1,287km) east of New York city. The passenger ship, it was reasoned, could just as easily have been an enemy warship carrying troops to invade New Jersey.

The event was stage-managed, with *New York Times* military expert Hanson W. Baldwin along for the ride and with approval being obtained in advance not merely from higher-ups but from the Italian cruise line.

With Major Caleb V. Haynes as flight commander and Lieutenant Curtis E. LeMay as lead navigator, the trio of Fortresses made a 4½-hour flight in poor weather which enabled them to materialize out of low cloud cover and 'buzz' the ocean liner. In those days intercepting a ship 800 miles out to sea was no easy feat and while passengers waved, a photographer in one B-17 took a photo of the other two silver bombers streaking by *Rex* at mast height. The picture appeared in no fewer than 1,800 newspapers and magazines to publicize the Air Corps' growing power. Olds and his boss, General Frank M. Andrews (chief of GHQ Air Force), were told in no uncertain terms, however, that they had trespassed in an area hitherto reserved for the Navy.

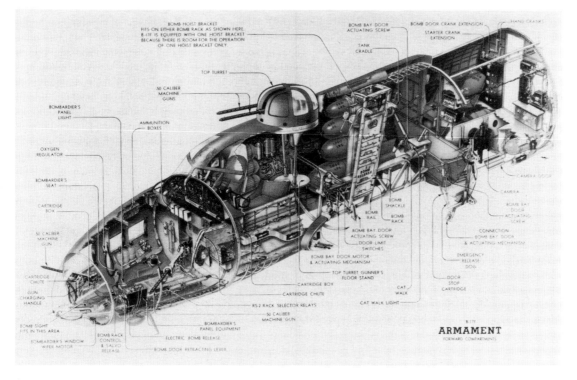

BOMB HOIST BRACKET
FITS ON EITHER BOMB RACK AS SHOWN HERE
B-17F IS EQUIPPED WITH ONE HOIST BRACKET
BECAUSE THERE IS ROOM FOR THE OPERATION
OF ONE HOIST BRACKET ONLY.

BOMB BAY DOOR
ACTUATING SCREW

BOMB DOOR CRANK EXTENSION

STARTER CRANK
EXTENSION

HAND CRANK

TANK
CRADLE

TOP TURRET

.50 CALIBER
MACHINE
GUNS

BOMBARDIER'S
PANEL
LIGHT

AMMUNITION
BOXES

OXYGEN
REGULATOR

BOMBARDIER'S
SEAT

CARTRIDGE
BOX

.50 CALIBER
MACHINE
GUN

CARTRIDGE
CHUTE

GUN
CHARGING
HANDLE

BOMB SIGHT
FITS IN THIS AREA

BOMBARDIER'S WINDOW
WIPER MOTOR

BOMB RACK
CONTROL
& SALVO
RELEASE

BOMBARDIER'S
PANEL EQUIPMENT

ELECTRIC BOMB RELEASE

BOMB DOOR RETRACTING LEVER

RS-2 RACK SELECTOR RELAYS

.50 CALIBER
MACHINE GUN

CARTRIDGE CHUTE

CARTRIDGE BOX

BOMB BAY DOOR MOTOR
& ACTUATING MECHANISM

BOMB BAY DOOR
ACTUATING SCREW

DOOR LIMIT
SWITCHES

BOMB
RAIL

BOMB
SHACKLE

BOMB
RACK

TOP TURRET GUNNER'S
FLOOR STAND

CAT WALK LIGHT

CAT
WALK

CAMERA DOOR

CAMERA

BOMB BAY
DOOR
ACTUATING
SCREW

CONNECTION
BOMB BAY DOOR
& ACTUATING MECHANISM

EMERGENCY
RELEASE
ROD

DOOR
STOP
CARTRIDGE

B-171

**ARMAMENT**
FORWARD COMPARTMENTS

**Left and right:** Cutaways showing interior of the B-17F. (Boeing)

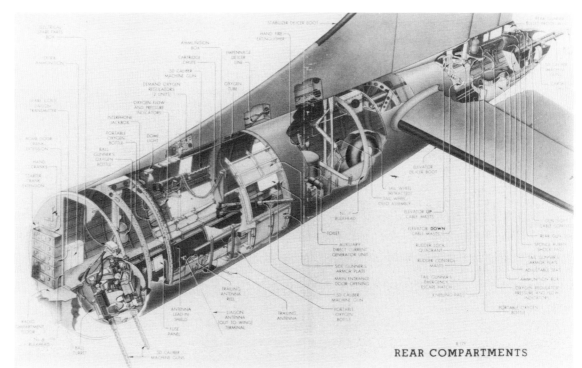

Early reaction to the natural metal finish which replaced camouflage on the B-17 was that it was 'too clean' and that somehow it could not be a real bomber subject to the punishments of war. These early B-17Gs from the Boeing-Seattle plant are lined up at Laredo AAF Base, Texas, on 20 December 1944. (USAF)

**REAR COMPARTMENTS**

Political battles between admirals and bomber generals were an integral part of the history of airpower both before and after World War II and some of them were utterly shameless, with the needs of a nation coming second to the parochial interests of a single armed service. Not even the most forward-thinking Air Corps leaders could have fully understood that long-range bombing was becoming a new kind of warfare, rather than an adjunct to the traditional ways of fighting. As late as 1939 budget requests were still being justified with the notion that the purpose of a bomber was to hit enemy vessels offshore. Admirals and many generals tended to think of bombers as utterly useless. Bomber advocates such as Andrews, Olds, Colonel Hugh Knerr and Major Ira C. Eaker tended to portray bombers as almost invulnerable, able to outrun fighters and defend themselves with criss-crossing streams of machine-gun fire.

## 'B' Model Fortress

The B-17B entered service in 1939 and was the fastest as well as the highest-flying bomber in the world. Also in 1939 a further 39 Flying Fortresses were ordered under the designation B-17C. These offered heavier armour, more defensive armament (machine-guns being emphasized by the Air Corps as the way to protect a bomber formation from enemy fighters) and tipped the scales at 49,650lb (22,521kg), a significant increase over the 43,000lb (19,505kg) weight of earlier Fortresses. Increasingly,

the use of massed formations of heavy bombers, fully capable of defending themselves (with a total of nine machine-guns on the B-17C), was central to Army bombing doctrine. It was to be a long time before anyone took enemy interceptors seriously, and even longer before anyone thought about fighter escort.

As far back as 1934, in tests between Martin B-12 bombers and Boeing P-26 fighters, it had been proved – or so everyone thought – that the larger warplanes could fly so fast that interceptors could not engage on any practical terms. The *Rex* incident, and the intense war games carried out in the US soon afterwards, seemed to prove that a bomber like the B-17 had a key role to play in defending the country and preparing for any future war. But hardly anyone paid attention.

For five years (1935–40) bomber advocates within the Army Air Corps were silenced and development of the B-17 (and other bombers) was handicapped at every turn. It was one of the stupidest periods in American military history and it was surely respon-

sible for the debacle at Pearl Harbor, where land-based long-range Flying Fortress patrols might have foiled the Japanese surprise attack. In an isolationist society, which had never really come to terms with the terrible casualties of the previous world war, it was official US policy that the battleship remained the first line of American defence while aircraft were to be used for 'scouting and reconnaissance'. No one, then or later, entertained the idea that the nation's armed forces should prepare not for defence but for offence.

Thus it occurred, in the summer before Munich, that the Army top brass rejected the Air Corps' request for further B-17 bombers; the Air Corps had requested 108 of the four-engined Flying Fortresses. A year later, in September 1939, while Hitler's panzers were overrunning Poland, the Air Corps had just nineteen of the bombers in its inventory. Of the 39 B-17C Fortresses ordered, 20 were exported to Britain where, as RAF Fortress Is, they had a brief moment on stage which was mismanaged and proved disastrous. Eventually their numbers were

Two views of a B-17G Fortress, aircraft 42-38091, manufactured under licence by Douglas at Long Beach and apparently on a delivery flight in early 1943. At about the time bars were added to the US national insignia, the Army Air Forces decided to dispense with camouflage paint. Soon after this Fortress was delivered, bombers came off the production line in natural metal finish. (USAF)

reduced to about nine and these were transferred to Coastal Command and the Middle East.

The B-17D Fortress, 42 of which were ordered in 1940, introduced a new electrical system and engine-cowling cooling gills. The B-17D was in service at Pearl Harbor when 30 were destroyed at Hickam Field, Honolulu, and at Clark Field in the Philippines. Equipped with a gun/observation position in a ventral bathtub and flush waist gun positions instead of blisters, the B-17D still had the familiar pointed tail of early Fortresses.

That month was the onset of war for Americans and the first few days of combat – sprung upon a very surprised and unprepared people – almost wiped out the air arm's inventory of Fortresses. Five were caught on the ground and destroyed during the Pearl Harbor attack. In the Philippines, where further surprise attacks fell on those who bore the brunt of early resistance against the Japanese, B-17D Fortresses carried out the first American bombing raid of the war on 10 December 1941 – a decidedly lacklustre effort aimed at the Japanese invasion fleet

bound for Luzon. Apart from the saga of Captain Colin B. Kelly, whose name will reappear shortly, the mission was in fact unsuccessful. Shortly afterwards the surviving Fortresses were redeployed to Australia where they were operated by units such as the 43rd Bombardment Group at Maceeba, Queensland.

It was the B-17E model which first showed the definitive shape of the Fortress. The B-17E introduced a far larger and differently shaped tail, with a huge dorsal fin and long-span tailplane giving better control and stability at high altitude. Although earlier Fortresses had been considered heavily armed for the standard of the time, B-17E defensive armament was vastly im-proved, with paired 0.50in (12.7mm) machine-guns in a power turret of new design located behind the flight crew deck, in a ventral turret in line with the trailing edge of the wing, and in the new manned position at the tail. In all, the B-17E had no fewer than twelve guns (all but two of them 0.50in size); another pair of guns could be fired by hand from the roof of the radio compartment, two smaller 0.30in (7.62mm) guns were positioned with the bombardier in the nose, and a single hand-held gun was located at each waist position.

The Air Corps – its name soon to be changed to the US Army Air Forces (USAAF) – was counting far too much on the heavy gun armament to protect its bombers from enemy fighters. The introduction of a flexible tail gun to the B-17E helped rectify a serious flaw in the design of the Fortress, which was vulnerable to fighter attack from astern (to say nothing of its susceptibility to head-on passes), but training exercises and bomber doctrine still called for formations of Fortresses to fly and fight alone. When the United States entered the war, the Republic P-47 Thunderbolt and North American P-51 Mustang were all moving ahead on designers' drawing-boards and in expanding aircraft factories, but no one had thought that a Thunderbolt or

Mustang – or the Lockheed P-38 Lightning, which had already flown – might be charged with escorting bombers.

The B-17E model was more heavily armoured than previous Fortresses, an improvement which was to be even more important than the added guns, and its gross weight had risen to 54,000lb (24,494kg). On a hot day, getting a fully loaded Fortress into the sky from a short runway could be a real challenge. The increase in weight (and drag!) also lowered cruising speed from 231 to 210mph (340km/h). In all, 512 examples of the B-17E version were built, including 45 which went to Britain as the Fortress IIA.

In April 1942 the B-17F introduced many improvements, including a frameless plexiglass nose which in later versions had two 0.50in (12.7mm) guns in left and right 'cheek' mountings. First flown on 30

May 1942, the 'F' model's gross weight went up to 65,000lb (29,484kg), with a bomb load for short ranges of 20,800lb (9,435kg), although in actual combat conditions the bomb load would rarely exceed 5,000lb (2,268kg). Boeing built 2,300 B-17Fs and a further 605 were built by Douglas and 500 by Lockheed-Vega as additional production lines for the Fortress were opened up.

The first combat operations involved early Fortresses, some of them B-17Ds, which proved vulnerable to Japanese fighters in the Pacific. At a time when Japan reigned supreme and the Mitsubishi A6M2 Zero-sen fighter was viewed with awe, Fortresses turned out to be relatively unmanoeuvrable while under attack; their 0.30in (7.62mm) machine-gun armament proved to have too few barrels and too little range, and they were not able to outrun Japanese fighters in the way their designers had

A superb view of Flying Fortresses over Rapid City Army Air Base, South Dakota, during the war. The combination of camouflage and natural metal produces a dramatic effect. A B-17G manufactured in Seattle, aircraft 42-102755, is one of the aircraft in this gaggle. (USAF)

expected. The lack of an effective tail gun was an omission which seemed, to many, almost criminal. Since no new or original knowledge was required to design such a gun installation, why hadn't it been done? The answer was that the Air Corps hadn't specified a need for it.

## Bomber Generals

Many of the same men who had developed the B-17 in the late 1930s took the new bomber to war in 1942. Using the B-17E and B-17F (and eventually adding the definitive B-17G model), the 8th Air Force built up its early strength in England. Brigadier-General Ira Eaker and a small party moved into 'Pinetree' (code-name for the former Wycombe Abbey School for girls which had now become VIII Bomber Command headquarters) and set their minds to the question of how best to commit the Fortress to action against the seemingly unbeatable Third Reich. Eaker was the first commanding general of the fledgling 8th Air Force and strongly believed that the US should conduct daylight bombing and 'sell' the idea to highly sceptical British leaders, who, following painful experience, now considered that the long-range air war was best fought at night.

There were many younger officers to add talent to the growing pool of American bomber men, among them Captain Beirne Lay and Major S. S. ('Sy') Bartlett who were now busy plotting to bomb the Reich but who, years later, would co-author the film-movie 'Twelve O'Clock High'. Major General Carl ('Tooey') Spaatz arrived on 20 June 1942 to add his sizeable talents to the unfolding scheme to bomb the Continent. Later in the war Spaatz became 8th Air Force commander and continued the campaign against occupied Europe begun by Eaker.

To all of them, general or captain or private, special emotions were aroused by the sight of a B-17 Fortress operating from bases with names from antiquity like Molesworth, Grafton Underwood and Wickstead Heath. Not all the emotions were suitable for mixed company, especially those of an irate maintenance sergeant who discovered that the Fortress could not be taxied through knee-deep bogs of mud. But the special inspiration of the B-17, which had been evident to some during the development years, did not lose its effect in England. Staff Sergeant Frederick B. Newman remembers an aircrew stretching the rules by buzzing Molesworth at low level:

'They were charged-up, these guys, because they wanted to be turned loose, and while we were bedding down the aircraft they took every chance to show off their aggressive flying style. This one pilot

brought his Flying Fortress in low and fast, I swear no more than 100 feet (30m) off the ground, and pulled some sharp turns and climb-outs. It was like going to an air show without buying a ticket. I don't think his manoeuvres had much practical application in wartime and I *know* they weren't allowed by regulation, but it was impressive. The pilot was never punished in any way.'

The first combat mission was flown on 17 August 1942 by twelve B-17Es of the 97th Bomb Group against a marshalling yard near Rouen, France. Brigadier General Ira Eaker piloted the lead bomber, B-17E number 41-9023, christened 'Yankee Doodle'. Group commander Colonel Frank Armstrong exercised the maxim known as RHIP (rank has its privileges) and usurped the pilot's seat of another B-17E nicknamed 'Butcher Shop' from Major Paul W. Tibbets, who went along on the mission in the right-hand seat and wrote a letter about it to his mother, Enola Gay – after whom he was to name another Boeing bomber later in the war. The mission was a modest one, with no dramatic results, and it was in part a Press event with some 30 journalists on hand to cover the safe return of the bomber force.

It was hardly the turning point in the conflict, but the Fortress was impressive, no doubt about it. In its olive-drab camouflage, it was a kind of testimony to the ultimate in the Industrial Age, a collection of steel and other metals which had somehow been moulded into a rather streamlined shape and which, for reasons that might not have been clear to Isaac

Newton, actually flew. In later years men would begin a post-Industrial period, but in 1942 the tanks, battleships and bombers coming from stateside production lines were the ultimate in machinery. Not every aspect of the Fortress's design was well liked, but no one could stand next to the bomber and not be impressed.

## Mystery Blast

Not everything that happened to the Fortress was related to the design of the aircraft. Once in a while something happened that defied explanation. On 27 May 1943 an explosion rocked the bomber base at Alconbury, home of the 95th Bomb Group, sending black plumes of smoke into the sky and killing eighteen men instantly. In an instant B-17F 42-29685 disappeared from the face of the earth, leaving behind only a glazed black surface where the heat of the blast had scorched the ground. GIs picked up an ordnance officer some distance away who was unbruised, unmarked, uncut by flying metal, but dead nonetheless, apparently killed by the concussion. At least four more Fortresses were badly damaged, one of them, 42-29008, seemingly broken in two. The unprecedented blast, never really explained and never repeated, was apparently the result of accidental detonation of 500lb (227kg) bombs, but the actual cause was never determined and remains a matter of speculation.

While the Fortress was beginning to make its

Flying Fortresses at war. The image of bomber swarms, riding their own contrails at high altitude and unleashing bombs over target, is not original and not new – nor is the second set of white vapour trails carved into the picture by 'little friends', the Mustangs or Thunderbolts escorting the bombers. But these portrayals of the B-17 at war have a timelessness to them, as if the role of men and machine is etched permanently, no one wanting to discard or forget how it looked when history was happening. (USAF)

mark in the European conflict and, to a lesser extent, serving in the Pacific, the manufacturer moved ahead with the definitive 'G' model of the aircraft.

Design of the B-17G took into account the sheer terror felt by US airmen when Messerschmitt and Focke-Wulf fighters engaged them in frontal attacks. As one put it, 'It was like the devil staring you in the face' when a bomber cruising at 270mph (435km/h) was engaged from the front by a fighter attacking at 400mph (640km/h); when the two aircraft were head-to-head they converged at a combined speed of 670mph (1,075km/h) and more than one 8th Air Force crewman readily admitted that such a blurred, high-speed, eyeball-to-eyeball encounter was more than his psyche could handle. The B-17G addressed this situation by adding a 'chin' turret with two more guns (first seen on B-17F-115-BO production aircraft), making a total of thirteen guns, all of 0.50in (12.7mm) calibre. (The odd number was the result of only one gun being fitted in the roof of the radio compartment.)

The B-17G was in fact the final, definitive production model of the Fortress and no fewer than 8,680 of them were delivered; 112 were transferred to Britain as the Fortress III.

At least one other Fortress variant entered the picture in May 1943 when a B-17E was experimentally fitted with four 1,425hp Allison V-1710-89 liquid-cooled engines and subjected to a flight test programme under the designation XB-38. Some improvement in performance was noted (although the liquid-cooled engines were sorely needed for fighters like the P-38 and P-40), but in the end no decision was made to open a production line of B-38As. At the very time it was showing promise, the sole XB-38 was destroyed in a fire in June 1943.

The Lockheed-Vega conversion of a B-17F aimed at producing a flying gun platform led to the XB-40, followed by some twenty YB-40s. This version was the ultimate Fortress in a sense, intended as a 'convoy fighter' to bring guns to bear on opposing fighters (it carried no bomb load). Armament varied from one airframe to another, but the YB-40 was indeed a veritable 'Fortress', a typical warload being as many as 30 weapons ranging from 0.30in (7.62mm) machine-guns to 20mm cannon. YB-40s escorted B-17s on combat missions beginning with a raid on St Nazaire in May 1943. The aeroplanes flew from Alconbury and other locations, achieving some success, but their added weight prevented them from staying in formation with B-17 bombers. This interesting variant of the Fortress eventually ended up stateside, carrying out a training role as the TB-40.

Cargo variants of the Fortress were designated XC-108 and C-108A.

## Crew Composition

As with any of the American bombers which dominated airpower during the second global conflict, the B-17 was essentially a long narrow metal

tube into which men were jammed in positions far from optimum for human comfort. The pilot (who was also the aircraft commander) usually got most of the credit or blame for whatever happened, but it took all ten men to make a bombing mission succeed and the pilot was not always the most important of the lot.

Normally the crew of a B-17 Fortress consisted of pilot, co-pilot, bombardier and navigator (these four being officers), flight engineer, top turret gunner, radio-operator, ball turret gunner, and two waist gunners. One of these doubled as tail gunner. It was the ball turret gunner, hunched in his narrow confines beneath the belly of the Fortress, who suffered the most discomfort and, if the B-17 was hit, was likely to have the least chance of baling out.

A typical mission could last six hours. Cramped confines and bulky clothing prevented most crewmen from wearing seat-pack parachutes, so when the alarm bell rang it was madness struggling to 'get out' – and if the bomber fell into a spin, the resulting centrifugal forces could pin the men helpless inside the fuselage. Flying a B-17 mission was also an extremely cold business. Frostbite, which could sometimes be exacerbated by a man's own sweat, inflicted injuries on almost every mission. Windblast coming through the open waist gun positions could reach 60deg below zero. The same bulky coveralls and electrically heated boots and gloves which hampered bale-outs were rarely enough to protect from the cold. Worst of all, an oxygen mask could itch and chafe at high altitude and the rubber bladder of the mask could freeze above 20,000ft (6,096m), causing hypoxia and sometimes death.

In contrast, in the Pacific where the B-17 Fortress is less well remembered, men flew combat missions over New Guinea bare-chested, wearing knee-length shorts, usually forsaking personal armour on the theory that the heat was a worse enemy than Japan's fighter pilots, who had a superb machine in the Zero but never managed to threaten bomber crews to the same extent that their Luftwaffe brethren did. This is not to say that Fortress crews in the Pacific War were having a picnic. Typical is the much-ballyhooed legend of Philippines-based Captain Colin P. Kelly Jr, martyred in the American Press as one of the first true heroes of the war for attacking the battleship *Haruna* (which he didn't), sinking the enemy vessel (which he didn't, either) and receiving the Medal of Honor (which never happened). Kelly was, in fact, a fine pilot who did attack and probably damaged a smaller Japanese ship, then pushed his B-17 through vicious swarms of attacking Zero fighters, helped his crew bale out after the Zeros had inflicted mortal damage, and lost his own life saving his crew.

In the Mediterranean Theatre of Operations where the 12th Air Force operated the B-17 (2nd, 97th, 99th and 301st Bombardment Groups), fighter opposition was more sporadic but the risks remained high. One enlisted gunner had an administrative problem which caused him to miss a take-off from the dusty airbase at Oudjda, Tunisia. His B-17 with the remainder of the crew aboard veered sharply to the right, reason unknown, dipped a wing, and exploded. All aboard died.

Death, of course, came in various ways, and while Fortresses soon appeared in North Africa, at Midway, Guadalcanal and other places, it was the daylight bombing campaign in Europe that asked the most of the B-17 and the men who flew it. On 28 July 1943 one such bomber, nicknamed 'Ruthie II' after pilot First Lieutenant Robert L. Campbell's wife, was part of a deep strike force attacking the Focke-Wulf works at Oschersleben 90 miles (144km) from Berlin, when the grim reaper took his toll. Luftwaffe fighters making those highly perilous head-on attacks managed to hit 'Ruthie' with gunfire, crippling the oxygen supply to the gunners in the aft fuselage. One shell struck Campbell in the head, inflicting a mortal wound.

The co-pilot was First Lieutenant John C. Morgan, a veteran of the Royal Canadian Air Force despite his Texas origins. Morgan took the controls, struggled to keep the bomber on course for the target, and at the same time administered help to badly wounded crewmen, one of whom had had an arm ripped off at the socket. Pressing his attack with a blinding wind rushing in through broken plexiglass, Morgan succeeded in completing the bomb run under heavy fire and also achieved the near-impossible task of nursing the badly damaged 'Ruthie' all the way back to England, bringing the plane in with hundreds of shell holes and empty fuel gauges. Single-handed, Morgan had pressed the war to the manufacturers of the very Fw 190 fighter which endangered his buddies so much. He became a recipient of the highest American award for valour, the Medal of Honor. Morgan's Medal of Honor aircraft was a B-17F-70-B0, serial 42-29802, coded 'JW-C', of the 326th Bomb Squadron, 92nd Bomb Group.

As the American daylight campaign was pressed against the Nazi-occupied Continent, there was room for heroism by many. The 17 August 1943 Schweinfurt-Regensburg raid, launched under heavy fog conditions and sent into the face of determined German fighter opposition, was a turning point. Of 124 aircraft that crossed the enemy coast heading towards Regensburg (belonging to the 94th, 95th, 96th, 100th, 385th, 388th and 390th Bombardment

Even on the ground, with no propellers turning, the Fortress evoked thoughts of beauty and grace. Camouflaged B-17G-30-BO 42-31828 of the 325th Bomb Squadron, 92nd Bomb Group, at an unidentified airfield in June 1943. (via Norman Taylor)

B-17G-65-BO Flying Fortress 43-37613, a product of Boeing's Seattle plant belonging to the 91st Bomb Group, lies on its belly at Bassingbourn, England, alias Station 121. This time the cause may not have been German flak. Another time a belly landing might prove even more destructive. (via Norman Taylor)

Groups), no fewer than 24 were lost in action – a reminder, once again, of the staggering cost when large numbers of bombers with ten men aboard fall from the sky.

But this was only the beginning. The second wave of 230 B-17 Fortresses assaulting the Schweinfurt ball-bearing works (coming from the 91st, 92nd, 303rd, 305th, 306th, 351st, 379th, 381st and 384th Bombardment Groups) flew into some of the most determined opposition yet to be mounted by the Luftwaffe's intrepid Messerschmitt and Focke-Wulf pilots. Thirty-six B-17s were downed in combat with 371 men aboard; a further nineteen were so badly damaged as to be written off after the raid.

## Concept Redeemed

There were better days ahead. As men like Spaatz, Eaker, LeMay, Major General William Kepner and Major General Haywood ('Possum') Hansell progressed along the learning curve – and as the size of the air armada in the British Isles grew – missions were flown against heavily defended targets with only minimal losses.

The original idea of employing the firepower of a bomber to protect it from fighters proved very effective once the 8th Air Force adopted a LeMay-devised formation which enabled numerous B-17s to combine the firepower of their guns. The development of long-range escort fighters, especially the P-51 Mustang, proved far more important in cementing tactics which overcame German resistance. Different views existed about evasive actions to avoid flak and fighters, and no satisfactory answers were ever found for the relatively low speed and vulnerability of the bombers, to say nothing of the vulnerability of any B-17 that had the misfortune to stray from the pack – but the development of tactics and techniques was accompanied by another American phenomenon which helped to win the air war. Sheer numbers. It was the perseverance, the staying power, the courage of men, and the vast numbers of four-engined bombers that ultimately brought the victory in Europe.

And what of the widespread belief that lives were wasted, bombing was ineffective, and claims for success were overrated? When it was over, many said that the bombing had been ineffective. Legitimate dispute will always exist over the accuracy of bombs aimed via Norden optical sight, dropped while under pressure from flak and fighters, and subject to vagaries of wind and temperature. Many German industries responded to the bombing campaign by dispersing (and, to an extent, surviving). The fact remains: the B-17 and the campaign it led

Vega-built B-17G-VE Fortress 44-85818, underbelly radar protruding, on a mission. The BTO (bombing through overcast) or 'Mickey' radar encumbered the ventral ball turret position and made possible very precise high-altitude bombing in poor weather. (USAF)

over Europe dealt a punishing blow which hastened the Allied victory. Responding to the sceptics, the British historian Roger Freeman tells Flying Fortress veterans, 'You were part of the decisive Allied victory over the very worst tyranny that man has ever known.'

Of the one and one half million US tons of bombs dropped on European targets, 640,036 were dropped by B-17s while 452,508 fell from Consolidated B-24 Liberators and 463,544 came from all other US aircraft types combined. All such numbers must, of course, be viewed with a critical eye, but the orders of magnitude convey a meaningful message.

The European war will reappear in the narrative which follows. Its turning points are well known: the first daylight raid over Berlin (something Hermann Goering had said could never happen); the successful use of the P-51 Mustang to escort bomber formations and protect them from enemy fighters, and finally the time of triumph when mighty waves of American bombers ruled the air over the Reich. Near the end of the conflict in May 1945 there was little German opposition of any kind, and the bombers changed their role to dropping food to refugees as no standing military targets remained. In the meanwhile, of course, the casualties were enormous, the sacrifice was great, and uncommon valour was a daily attribute. No fewer than fourteen

B-17 crewmen followed John Morgan in receiving the decoration Americans view with a special awe, the Medal of Honor.

The strategic bombing war was fought by RAF Lancasters, Stirlings and Halifaxes, which succeeded the earlier bombers used in Britain's first two years of war. The American portion of the conflict was carried home to the Reich by Havocs, Marauders, Liberators, Invaders – and might well have seen Superfortresses, had time not run out for Hitler and his cohorts. But the brunt of the war, and the focus of the popular vision, will always be on the Boeing B-17 Flying Fortress.

The vision of the Boeing company's planners, the trial and error of Air Corps doctrine men in the late 1930s, the pioneering efforts of officers such as Robert Olds and Frank Armstrong, all paid off with handsome dividend when the B-17 Flying Fortress went from being an experimental concept to one of the most numerous bomber types ever built. The original purpose of using the bomber to defend an isolated America shielded by oceans gave way to the terrible danger and unbelievable determination of the daylight bombing campaign against the Reich. There would continue to be many uses for the B-17 after war's end, but in the pitched battles of the war itself the B-17's record of achievement was without peer. The Boeing 299 had come a long way.

The last trip. Built by Douglas at Long Beach, the USAF's B-17G-DL Fortress 44-83624 is towed across the river near Wright-Patterson AFB, Ohio, in 1971, en route to its final resting place. The aircraft is now on permanent display at the museum. (USAF)

# A-20 Havoc and A-26 Invader

The strategic bombing offensive, fought at high altitude in freezing temperatures by men in four-engined bombers, was a bigger, broader version of the war fought by men in small, nimble bombers at lower level. And bombers they were. Their war was, in one sense, far more personal, for crews of the twin-engined light bombers were often face-to-face with their enemies. Every theatre of war, every continent, saw action by the Douglas A-20 Havoc – not the most important bomber of the war but among the most popular – an aeroplane which owed its origins mostly to personal and corporate initiative.

The A-20 Havoc was the American offspring of the Model 7B designed in 1938 by Jack Northrop and Edward A. Heinemann of Douglas Aircraft. The two men were leaders and innovators and their design reflected their ambition. The US Army had not even specified twin engines, let alone tricycle landing gear, on an attack aircraft. When Northrop and Heinemann won a contract to build a prototype, it came to them reluctantly and when their aircraft materialized, it showed little promise of the future to come. The Douglas 7B was first flown at the Douglas plant in El Segundo, California, on 26 October 1938. Powered by two Pratt & Whitney R-1830C engines of 1,100hp each, it was a snub-nosed, scoop-bellied machine and it was not long for the world.

Like many American warplanes of the period, this predecessor of the A-20 went to a foreign air arm. It was January 1940 when France's Armée de l'Air began operating the production Douglas DB-7 attack bomber with its 19th and 32nd Groups (comprising the equivalent of four squadrons, GB I/19, II/19, I/32 and II/32), at first in Morocco and later in Metropolitan France. Even then, of course, it was too late

A-20G Havoc attack bomber 43-10208 on a combat mission late in the war. The rudder markings identify the 647th Bomb Squadron, 410th Bomb Group, IX Bomber Command, European Theatre. The squadron went into combat in May 1944 with late-model A-20Gs and was later equipped with the elegant Douglas A-26 Invader. (via David A. Anderton)

A-20G Havoc 43-9942 of the 643rd Bomb Squadron, nicknamed 'Chattanooga Belle', over Germany late in the war. Bombs hang beneath the wing outboard of the engine nacelles. The Havoc was not renowned for long range, but it flew and fought in every theatre of the war. (via Norman Taylor)

for France to prevent the German armies from overrunning her territory. The British were interested in the DB-7B as the production aircraft was now called, and the US Army belatedly showed interest as well. The result was to be a confusion of names and identities, between the company term DB-7 and the USAAF designation A-20, and between the names Boston and Havoc which the RAF gave the type; in British service Boston was used for the bomber variant and Havoc for the night fighter. Later in the war the USAAF adopted the name Havoc for its aircraft.

The RAF initially ordered 150 airframes in a contract dated 20 February 1940, later raised the figure to 300, and eventually obtained no fewer than 781. France and Belgium had ordered, respectively, 200 and 18 DB-7 Boston I aircraft, and France later ordered 249 DB-7A Boston IIs. Britain also ordered improved DB-7B Boston IIIs. None of the Belgian machines was delivered and after France had fallen, many aircraft of the French contracts were taken over by the RAF.

## Attack Bomber

The aircraft which most Americans know simply as the A-20 Havoc became a reality when Heinemann's design team refined the shape of their prototype. The production Havoc for American forces, one of the first combat aeroplanes to have a nosewheel, was a sleek and streamlined machine, sensibly configured and pleasing to the eye. If not exactly easy for a pilot to convert to, it was a supremely practical aircraft. Pilots who had once believed that all flying machines had tailwheels suddenly found themselves sitting high and comfortable, their cockpit situated well forward of the arcs described by the twin propellers, able now, in a tricycle-gear machine, to taxi with no need for S-turns – their all-round vision nothing less than superb.

Clean lines and good visibility were fine, but the A-20 Havoc also had a handicap. Due to the narrowness of the fuselage, each crewman – always consisting of pilot and radio-operator/gunner and, on glass-nosed aircraft, a bombardier – was fixed in his own position aboard the bomber, unable to be in physical contact or exchange places with the others. If the pilot was incapacitated, the bombardier in the nose and gunner in his dorsal compartment had no choice but to hitch up their parachutes and bale out. For cosmetic purposes, some A-20 Havocs were built with token flight controls in the rear seat. These consisted only of stick, rudder pedals and throttle, and the gunner was unlikely actually to fly the Havoc even if the pilot remained able to coach him over the intercom.

While it looked and felt like the forebear of a new generation, the A-20 Havoc was conventional in design – a slender, aluminium alloy semi-monocoque fuselage and a single-spar, aluminium alloy wing with fabric-covered control surfaces. Northrop and Heinemann apparently chose deliberately to enable the aircraft to carry a variety of armaments. The design called for fixed, forward-firing guns in various combinations while the rear gunner operated a flexible 0.303in machine-gun in both dorsal and ventral locations, each stocked with 500 rounds of ammunition. The aeroplane's tandem bomb bays could accommodate a normal load of 1,200lb (544kg) of bombs of various types, a typical A-20 being equipped with two vertical racks for six 100lb (45kg) bombs. Up to 2,000lb (908kg) of bombs could be carried over shorter distances.

## RAF Variants

In 1940 Britain's Royal Air Force, taking delivery of aircraft originally slated for France, decided to convert some Boston IIs to meet a pressing need for night fighters. Flame-damper engine exhausts, four forward-firing Browning 0.303in machine-guns and a single Vickers 'K' machine-gun were added to the basic design. As a night fighter or 'intruder', the interchangeable nose feature provided a means of installing detection equipment, including a powerful searchlight. A hopeful document by Douglas's T. R. Smith in 1942 told readers that the searchlight would not only point out the location of enemy aircraft but would 'blind the crews of enemy planes in order to get in the first shot'. Smith was apparently referring to the Helmore Turbinlite, a nose-mounted searchlight.

With No 23 Squadron, RAF, these low-level night intruders commenced sorties over Europe in the winter of 1940–41. Nicknamed variously as 'Rangers' and 'Moonfighters', these aircraft were officially designated the Havoc I (Intruder). Later machines with no fewer than twelve 0.303in nose guns and with airborne interception radar became the Havoc II (Night Fighter).

In a surge of fighting just after the Battle of Britain, these variants of the DB-7 design served the RAF very effectively. In December 1940 No 93 Squadron began to receive Havoc Is modified to carry the 'Pandora' Long Aerial Mine, which had first been used by the squadron's Harrows. When dropped, a parachute opened and from the device a long cable unwound, with an explosive charge at its end. The mines were strewn in the path of oncoming enemy bombers, with little success, although Sgt Wray in Havoc AX913 claimed a kill using this bizarre and short-lived method.

Outlandish may be the word for the 2,700 million candlepower searchlight devised by Wing-Com-

The Havoc (night fighter) and Boston (light bomber) series was widely used by the RAF. BZ377 is a Boston IIIA of No 88 Squadron and has a twin 0.303in (7.69mm) machine-gun mount for the upper rear gunner. (via Gordon Swanborough)

USAAF A-20 Havoc flying a mere 100ft (31m) above ground at Lae, New Guinea, skimming a road during a strafing attack on Japanese aircraft. The Havoc has just passed over a disabled Mitsubishi G4M bomber. Under the tree to the right of the Havoc and barely visible in the photo is a disabled 'Zero' fighter. (USAF)

mander W. Helmore for the nose of the Havoc II (Turbinlite) aircraft. Batteries were carried in the Havoc's bomb bay but because of their weight this night-fighter variant was unarmed. The Havoc was to home in on a German attacker and, at a range of 3,000ft (914m), illuminate it for accompanying Hurricanes – which eventually served side-by-side with the Havoc II (Turbinlite) in RAF squadrons. Ten such squadrons roamed the night using this combined 'search and kill' technique – and, it has been reported, frightening some attackers away – until December 1942 when radar-equipped Bristol Beaufighters and de Havilland Mosquitoes became available in the night interception role.

Creating a further confusion of names, Britain ordered DB-7B Boston IIIs which began to arrive in May 1941 and were locally modified as night fighters to become the Boston III (Intruder). These could carry a gun-pack containing four 20mm Hispano cannon beneath their fuselages. The Royal Canadian Air Force's No 418 Squadron at Debden, Essex, which was formed in November 1941, operated this type, as did No 605 Squadron, RAF.

## Global Havoc

The thin elegant Havoc had an easy claim to worldwide importance. A few DB-7Bs were shipped to Java in 1942 and some of these were captured by the Japanese; they were the first of an order for 80 DB-7Bs and DB-7Cs placed by the Dutch Navy for use in the then Netherlands East Indies. Russia became the most important single purchaser of the twin-engined bomber and eventually ordered no fewer than 3,125 Boston/Havoc aircraft (of which 2,901 arrived safely), compared with 1,962 operated by the US and nearly 1,800 by Britain. More than a few American pilots, in fact, experienced the adventure of their lives delivering Russia's A-20 Havocs via long and arduous ferry routes which touched points as far apart as Fairbanks, Alaska, and Teheran, Iran.

Some 69 Bostons, many of them earmarked at first for other recipients, reached Australia. All served with the RAAF's No 22 Squadron. Brazil was supplied with thirty-one A-20K Havocs in 1944–45 via Lend-Lease channels.

With its British user, the Boston/Havoc gradually lost its role as a night fighter and RAF Bomber Command began to oeprate the type on the offensive, including No 88 Squadron's search for the German battleship *Scharnhorst* in February 1942. Boston crews were limited by the range of their aircraft to targets in occupied France, Belgium and Holland although an occasional sortie took them deeper into the Third Reich. RAF Boston crews were especially valorous in the raid on the Philips Radio works at Eindhoven on 6 December 1942. Eventually the much faster Mosquito eclipsed the Boston as a light bomber in the European Theatre, although the twin-engined Douglas soldiered on performing other duties, such as smoke-laying off the Normandy Beaches in 1944. Boston IV and V models with power-operated dorsal turrets fought in the Middle East and Italy.

## USAAF Havocs

The US Army Air Forces' A-20, A-20A and A-20B Havocs saw little action. Douglas built one Model 7B prototype, 270 DB-7s (Boston I, II), 99 DB-7As (Boston III), 880 DB-7Bs (also Boston III), 63 A-20s, 143 A-20As, one XA-20B, and 808 A-20Cs. After the A-20C, production of Boston/Havoc aircraft was shifted from Douglas plants in El Segundo and Long Beach (and from Boeing, which built an additional 140 USAAF A-20Cs) and manufacture of the attack bomber was concentrated at the Douglas Santa Monica facility.

It was the A-20C which arrived in England in June 1942 with the USAAF's 15th Bomb Squadron, seeing action against the Continent and later in North Africa.

The designation A-20D was assigned to a proposal which was cancelled. The A-20E was a conversion from the A-20A of an experimental version of the Havoc, seventeen of which were built. The XA-20F was another conversion, with a 37mm nose gun, and only one was completed.

Combat squadrons including the 15th BS soon began to acquire the A-20G solid-nose model, which was by far the most numerous Havoc with 2,850 built. This version dispensed with a bombardier in favour of nose armament, eventually comprising six 0.50in guns. A few were converted into transports as

the CA-20G and flown by Air Transport Command. The similar A-20H model (412 built) had 1,700hp R-2600-29 engines and a few of these later became TA-30H trainers.

To the USAAF, the major operational versions of the Havoc were the A-20J (450 built) and A-20K (413 built), which returned to a glazed nose of a new and more streamlined frameless type. Some A-20Ks were painted all black for night interdiction missions. A few performed trainer duties as the TA-20K.

To complete the long story of Havoc variants, British night fighter successes seem to have inspired the USAAF to convert early A-20 Havocs to the P-70 night fighter standard. When British air interception radar became available, the very first A-20 (39-735) was modified in 1942 to become an XP-70. In rapid succession, fifty-nine A-20 aircraft were converted to P-70 standard, thirteen A-20Cs to P-70A-1s, and twenty-six A-20Gs to P-70A-2s. Later one A-20G equipped with SCR-720 radar became the sole P-70B-1, while no fewer than 105 aircraft in the A-20G and A-20J series were converted to P-70B-2s.

The P-70 had a crew of two, the second man operating the radar set and guiding the pilot to the interception point. Throughout the P-70 programme various attempts were made to refine and develop the night-fighting capability of the aircraft, but while these were going on Northrop – the firm to which designer Jack Northrop had defected in 1938 – was designing its own twin-engined night fighter from the ground up. The Northrop product, the P-61 Black Widow, offered performance advantages over the P-70. The P-70 ended up being used primarily for training, although a few saw combat in the Pacific.

The photo-reconnaissance designation F-3 was assigned to camera-carrying Havocs. A sole A-20 airframe (39-741) became the XF-3 prototype. Two other early A-20s (39-745 and -748) became service-

Credited to the long-defunct Acme news agency on 26 March 1943 but possibly taken at a much earlier date, this view depicts camouflaged Douglas A-20 Havoc light bombers in unusual desert camouflage scheme taxi-ing for take-off in Tunisia. (USAF)

test YF-3s. No fewer than 46 A-20J and A-20K airframes were fitted with photographic gear to become service F-3A aircraft. The designation O-53 was set aside for a revised A-20B to be used for battlefield observation, but orders for 1,489 of these were cancelled when other priorities asserted themselves.

A single A-20A was delivered to the US Navy for tests and was designated BD-1. Eight A-20Bs went to the Navy as BD-2s and later joined the US Marine Corps as target tugs.

## Flying the A-20

When the first A-20s were delivered to the 3rd Bomb Group (Light) at Savannah, Georgia, in the spring of 1941, pilots knew that they had a responsive, highly manoeuvrable aircraft. They also realized quickly that the A-20 lacked both range and punch for heavy-hitting combat missions. This did not prevent

one pilot from describing the Havoc as 'sensational'. The transition from 'taildragger' aircraft to the nosewheel A-20 apparently evoked such sentiments. Visibility from the pilot's perch in the A-20 was excellent. Instruments, hydraulics and electrical systems were regarded as being of very good quality.

Havocs were delivered to the 27th Bomb Group before the outbreak of war and to the 58th Bomb Squadron which lost two aircraft at Hickam Field, Hawaii, during the 7 December 1941 Japanese attack. In the Pacific, the 3rd Bomb Group (Light) introduced the A-20 Havoc to combat. Some, modified by Major 'Pappy' Gunn of the 3rd Bomb Group to carry heavier nose armament, were used for low-level strafing in New Guinea.

Men who flew Havocs in the early days of the war were very experienced pilots, but they were soon augmented by the quickly trained cadre of fliers who were part of the air arm's rapid expansion. Even the

A-20 Havocs in formation for a raid against a German ammunition dump near Dieppe in September 1944. The twin-engined Havoc does not usually evoke images of massive bomber formations – Havocs often went on small-scale missions against convoys, trains and supply centres – but a formation of A-20s in flight could be an impressive sight. (USAF)

A-20 Havoc in foreground wears the black and white 'invasion stripes' added to aid recognition during the Normandy landings. The aircraft belongs to the 647th Bomb Squadron, 410th Bomb Group, which coincidentally had rudder markings to match the wing and fuselage stripes. The Havoc's Wright R-2600-3 Double Cyclone engines drove three-blade Hamilton Standard propellers. (via David Anderton)

least experienced, it seemed, could adjust to flying the Havoc.

The pilot entered the cockpit by opening a unique 7ft hinged, fold-out hatch and lowering himself into his seat. His cabin floor was foam-carpeted and all pipes and wires were protected by insulation, the roomy, armoured cockpit providing a kind of 'sports car' feel. On glazed-nose variants the bombardier sat well forward with a door in the bottom for entry and exit.

Apart from its taxi-ing qualities, the Havoc had in many respects the feel of a single-seat aircraft and could, indeed be flown by the pilot alone. The aircraft required a full take-off roll, which meant that it had to cover 5,000ft (1,525m) of runway to clear a height of 50ft (15m), but once having attained 110mph (177 km/h), it fairly leapt from the runway. The landing gear retracted quickly owing to the hydraulic accumulator and the initial rate of climb was impressive. Once aloft, the aircraft manoeuvred with great agility and, but for its limited top speed of around 335mph (540km/h), was in every respect a first-rate performer.

The tall single rudder was astonishingly responsive to the pilot's pressure on the pedals; a brief experiment with a twin-rudder tail unit on the 131st DB-7 Boston was found to offer no improvement. Some pilots found the Havoc a bit too powerful for easy control, at least on let-down and final approach, and felt that the brakes were not effective enough and needed changing too often. It was not a forgiving machine when it came to ending a fast landing in a full stop on a short runway.

## Havoc in Combat

The A-20 Havoc was never anything but a small, light, short-range aircraft capable of inflicting harm on the enemy but not to be compared with the mighty four-engined bombers which ranged deep into the Third Reich. Before the installation of extra fuel tanks, the Havoc was credited with a range of 1,090 miles (1,754km), but this figure may have been optimistic and no one ever claimed that the Havoc could carry very much, very far. A characteristic bomb load for a Havoc was four internally stowed bombs of up to 500lb (227kg) and four bombs of the same weight hanging from wing pylons. In time it became apparent that a few Havocs with this bomb load and with forward-firing guns could do a rather thorough job of pulverizing a German railroad yard or a Japanese port facility. Before the word 'tactical' became widespread in aviation parlance, the A-20 Havoc was a highly effective tactical bomber.

The A-20 seemed to have a special sense of purpose which was largely lacking in most of the other twin-engined bombers used so widely by air forces on both sides throughout the conflict. The others had their proponents and detractors – who, after all, can forget that the B-25 Mitchell bombed Tokyo? – but the A-20 seemed to possess a sleekness and a force that was not matched in the other designs, not even in the best from Messerschmitt and Mitsubishi.

The 3rd Bomb Group's 89th Squadron, which began operations at Port Moresby, New Guinea, on 30 August 1942, developed an in-field modification to lengthen the Havoc's combat radius. A 450 US gal fuel tank was installed in the upper bomb bay and four additional 0.50in (12.7mm) forward-firing machine-guns were installed in the nose, the bombardier's aiming panel being removed to allow the barrels to project. This kind of improvisation came easily to the highly individualistic mavericks of the 3rd Group, who were waging a catch-up war with no fewer than three aircraft types (their other squadrons had A-24 Dauntlesses and B-25C Mitchells). All 39 of their A-20As were so modified.

The 312th and 417th Bomb Groups which operated Havocs in the Pacific war came later in the war and operated later versions of the aircraft. As part of the Fifth Air Force, Havocs remained in the Pacific theatre until the war ended.

The P-70, that stopgap offspring from the Havoc which was intended solely to equip night-fighter squadrons until the P-61 Black Widow could be available, entered service just after Pearl Harbor with the 6th Night Fighter Squadron at Hickam Field. On 18 February 1943 a detachment of the squadron under Major Sydney F. Wharton moved to Guadalcanal with six P-70s.

The first air-to-air kill by a P-70 night fighter occurred over Guadalcanal on 18 April 1943 and was credited to Captain Earl C. Bennett and his radar operator, Corporal Edwin E. Tomlinson. The pair chased a Japanese Mitsubishi 'Betty' bomber across the island, weaving through friendly anti-aircraft fire, and shot it down.

Other attempts to score aerial victories were unsuccessful (although they may have deterred some nocturnal raids) and pilots found the P-70 unable to climb rapidly enough for real effectiveness. The 418th, 419th and 421st Night Fighter Squadrons arrived in the South-West Pacific in late 1943 and fought briefly with P-70s before converting to other types. Pilots of the 418th were so dissatisfied that they requested and obtained P-38H Lightnings with jury-rigged SCR-540 AI radar, long before the P-38M night fighter was developed. Colonel Carroll Smith, who became a top US night fighter ace, flew the P-70 before shifting to the P-61 Black Widow.

The small number of F-3A Havoc photo-reconnaissance aircraft actually saw rather wide use in combat and one F-3A was the first Allied aircraft to touch down at Itazuke air base in western Japan following the 15 August 1945 surrender. The crew might well have approached this experience with some trepidation as Itazuke was situated roughly mid-way between Hiroshima and Nagasaki!

Weathered and battered, a pair of Douglas A-20 Havocs fly through the skies of war, nearly blending with a diverse background of ridges and valleys. (USAF)

A-20 Havocs over occupied
Europe. (via David Anderton)

## European Fighting

From the outset of the conflict, the A-20 was highly sought after by commanders in both Europe and the Pacific. Whatever its shortcomings in terms of range and load-carrying capacity, it was ideal for the defensive, holding war the US was caught in. As historian Warren Thompson describes the aircraft, 'It could get in fast, do serious damage, and still have a chance of getting back to fight again.'

For a time there were simply not enough Havocs. In Europe personnel of the 15th Bomb Squadron arrived, without aircraft, as the spearhead of the Eighth Air Force in the summer of 1942. On 29 June 1942 one American crew manned an RAF Boston and flew with No 226 Squadron, RAF, on a combat mission. Early plans to operate three Havoc groups under the Eighth Air Force did not materialize, however, and the 15th in time transferred to Algeria, flying Bostons acquired from RAF stocks.

The 20th Bomb Group arrived in French Morocco in time to enter combat with its 58 A-20B Havocs on 13 December 1942. This unit remained with the Ninth Air Force in the Mediterranean and flew later Havocs until nearly the end of the war.

Together with the other twin-engined bombers of the era, the B-25 Mitchell (actually not an important player in Europe), B-26 Marauder and A-26 Invader, the Havoc was vital to the repeated bombings that came before, during and after the D-Day landings in Normandy. Not everything always worked as it should. Because they were tasked for low-level operations, many aircraft carried clusters of small bombs. The release mechanism, not previously tested in combat, tended to jam. Alternatively, bombs would be released when they should not, even when bomb bay doors were closed. Field modifications eventually resolved the problem, but many an A-20 Havoc returned to base with bomb bay doors torn off and some with bombs still dangling precariously from faulty shackles.

By July 1944 Havocs had a key role in assaulting the bridges across the River Seine near Paris. German crews effected hasty repairs only to see Havocs return to strike again.

This continued with the crossing of the Rhine and the move into German territory. Despite terrible weather, in five days over Christmas 1944, the 410th Bomb Group dropped 1,768 500lb (227kg) bombs on counter-attacking German armoured columns in the latter part of the Battle of the Bulge.

The Havoc was one of those aircraft which burst upon the scene, succeeded, and then quickly departed from view. A-20 Havocs were active following the German and Japanese surrenders, but within a couple of years after war's end they had been virtually stripped from inventory. As this volume was in preparation, what was believed to be the world's last flyable A-20 Havoc – now a 'warbird', or preserved civil aircraft – was lost in a crash. A few museum examples remain, including a fine one at the US Air Force Museum in Dayton, Ohio. But, especially considering the longevity of its successor, it is remarkable how brief the Havoc's service career was.

After the Allies had liberated Paris and set course for Berlin, they ran into snow. Operating from forward bases in late 1944 was demanding – and cold. Douglas A-20G Havoc 43-9365 seems to have nose wheel problems, hence the petrol drum used to hold the nose up amid a sea of white stuff. With bomb bay doors open and canopy top raised, this A-20G is receiving a thorough going-over by the mechanics, who were the unsung heroes of the bomber war. (via David Anderton)

A-20 Havocs being worked on in the snow, perhaps during the Battle of the Bulge. No fewer than seven men labour in the cold to remove snow or repair the aircraft. Air and ground crews had to be sensitive to the problem of wing icing, hence the constant efforts on the wing with a heavy broom. (via David Anderton)

Typical users of the A-20 Havoc in the European theatre included the 47th, 409th, 410th and 416th Bomb Groups. In its brief life, the A-20 Havoc made a profound impact on the conflict from beginning to end. But even while the war raged, Douglas engineers were already working on an improved version of the aircraft.

## A-26 Invader

Designed as a replacement for the Havoc without help from the departed Jack Northrop, but with a superb engineering team under Edward H. Heinemann's direction, the prototype XA-26 Invader (42-19504) took to the air on 10 July 1942 with Ben Howard at the controls. The outward appearance of the Invader changed little but the first machine differed from all others in having camouflage and large propeller spinners. The Invader was, to some spectators, the most elegant combat aircraft that the United States had built. It also embodied everything that had been learned with the Havoc and, in every respect, was an enormous improvement over the Havoc.

Heinemann began from the outset with three variants: the XA-26 (later A-26C) with a glazed nose for a bombardier; the A-26A night fighter with radar and four ventral-mounted 20mm cannon; and the XA-26B with a solid-gun nose for the ground-attack role. The night fighter version was short-lived but bombers churned from the Douglas production lines at Long Beach, California, and Tulsa, Oklahoma.

A truly graceful and pleasing aircraft, the Invader was also designed to be potent. Like its predecessor, the Invader was far from a long-range bomber but was exactly what the American forces needed for fighting within combat theatres. The A-26B (1,355 built) was armed with six 0.50in (12.7mm) machine-guns in the nose (later increased to eight), remotely controlled dorsal and ventral turrets each with two 0.50in (12.7mm) guns and up to ten more 0.50in (12.7mm) guns in underwing and underfuselage packs. Heavily armoured and able to carry up to 4,000lb (1,814kg) of bombs, the A-26B with its maximum speed of 355mph (571km/h) at 15,000ft (4,570m) was the fastest American bomber of World War II.

The A-26C Invader (1,091 built) introduced a bombardier's glazed nose. These, too, were manu-factured in Long Beach and Tulsa. Post-war conver-sions for reconnaissance, cargo and trainer duties were at various times introduced under the RB-26C, CB-26C and TB-26C designations. The XA-26D (one built) was an experimental variant with eight nose and six wing guns, all of 0.50in (12.7mm) calibre. The XA-26E (one built) was another experimental variant about which no data were released.

## Invader in Combat

Rushed into combat with the 553rd Bomb Squadron, Great Dunmow, England, by September 1944 and soon operating in France and Italy, the Invader was flying air-to-ground missions against the Germans before its bugs were ironed out. Pilots were delighted with its manoeuvrability and ease of handling.

It was never an easy aircraft to fly, however, and the Invader began to earn the affection of crews only after it started getting them out of trouble. The Invader began life with a needlessly complex and fatiguing instrument array, a weak nose gear that collapsed easily, and an early cockpit canopy that was almost impossible to hold in the open position for emergency bale-out. Time and attention resolved these problems and pilots took pride in mastering a demanding but effective bombing machine.

The people who kept tabs on numbers determined that the Invader had a normal range of 1,480 miles (2,380km) which seemed to indicate that a round-trip of around 600 miles (966km) was feasible. Under actual combat conditions, an aircraft never quite performed the way the brochure said, and it was more realistic to use the Invader against targets some 400 miles (643km) away from a friendly airfield. Again, like most of the bombers which fought in the global war, the Invader was more likely to be effective against an enemy's front lines and rear areas rather than his homeland, where the bigger four-engined bombers routinely went.

In the European theatre it is recorded that Invaders flew 11,567 sorties and dropped 18,054 tons of bombs. The Invader, whose predecessor had been converted into a night fighter, was also nimble enough to hold its own when challenged by fighters. Major Myron L. Durkee of the 386th Bomb Group at Beaumont, France, was credited with the 'prob-able' kill of a Messerschmitt Me 262 jet fighter on 19 February 1945.

Two Invaders were supplied briefly to the RAF, but Britain saw no benefit over other types then in service, such as her own de Havilland Mosquito.

In the Pacific war the Invader also progressed from an inauspicious beginning to a pinnacle of genuine achievement. With its 2,000hp Pratt & Whitney R-2800-27 Double Wasp engines and sea-

Typical of the blurred snapshot taken hastily by American fighting men in combat at forward air bases, this frontal shot seems to depict an A-26 Invader in France following the Normandy invasion. The Invader owed its clean lines to the earlier A-20 Havoc, from which its design was derived. Once in battle, however, even the cleanest bomber tended to acquire dents, smudges, and a general deterioration in appearance. (Frank Johnson)

Placed into USAAF archives on 27 March 1945, this view depicts Douglas A-26 Invader 41-39435 taking off, possibly on a stateside flight. Described by aviation authority David Anderton as one of the most elegant aircraft ever built, the A-26 was also one of the least-photographed, at least during the war years. Pilots loved the aircraft but might have done a better job in preserving a historical record of it. (USAF)

level speed of no less than 373mph (600km/h), the Invader was a potent anti-shipping and ground-attack weapon, but crews did not immediately take to it. A-20 pilots who had reigned supreme in their high single-seat cabins now found themselves with a YOT ('you over there') in the navigator's right-hand jump seat, essentially a co-pilot without controls.

There were other problems. When rockets and bombs were expended in unison in a low-level pass, debris from the rockets' explosions damaged the underside of the Invader. In the belief that the new machine was unsuited for low-level work, Fifth Air Force commander General George C. Kenney actually requested *not* to convert from the A-20 to the A-26. But conversions went ahead, the Invader also replacing B-25 Mitchells in some units.

## Pilot Talk

Being pilot of the A-26 Invader was a real experience. 'The airplane was graceful, potent and extremely unforgiving,' says Lt.-Col. Clifford Erly, who flew the Invader with the 416th Bomb Group in Europe.

Wide-track mainwheels and tricycle gear gave the Invader excellent ground-handling characteristics. On take-off it tended to 'eat up runway', says Erly, especially with a full ordnance load, 'but once you rotated and started to climb out, there was no ambiguity about it'. A revised instrument layout made the aircraft easy to handle and the Invader's tall single tail assured responsiveness in turns.

Visibility was not as good as on the A-20 because the engines were placed closer and farther forward, but the pilot remained able to see ahead and above remarkably well. Flight controls were provided for the pilot only (except in the post-war B-26K) and the

flight deck was roomy but cluttered. The YOT in the right seat, a navigator or flight engineer depending on the mission, was less comfortable than the pilot or the dorsal radio-operator who was also the gunner. The pilot had a heavy control yoke and throttles rather far forward for his right-hand reach. The bombardier's station on the glazed-nose Invader, reached through a nosewheel hatch, provided a Norden bombsight and a hand-held bomb-release button attached to a long cord to permit movement.

'Once rid of the bombs it was a real fighter,' says Erly. 'Not only were we almost as fast as any fighter in the air, we were almost as manoeuvrable. We had studies showing that at some altitudes, under some conditions, we could turn inside a Messerschmitt Me 109. I never heard of a fighter successfully engaging an A-26 because we had the choice. We could run away from him in the straightaway or we could turn and fight . . .'

In a sense the A-26 Invader gave the American air forces a weapon that neither the Germans nor the Japanese ever matched, and for which they never really had a credible defence. Other fast twin-engined bombers were employed by both sides during the war, and with no small amount of success on a variety of missions, but the Invader was one of the few to be designed after the outbreak of hostilities and it solidly out-performed everything in its league, as well as most fighters intended to defend against its onslaught.

Aviation expert David Anderton calls the A-26 Invader 'the most graceful twin-engined aircraft ever designed'. He adds, 'Not that the A-20 was ugly. It too, was an elegant aircraft. But that A-26 . . .'

Robert C. Mikesh, who flew the Invader in combat one war later, points out that many pilots and crews were not ready for its enormous power, speed, and climb rate. 'Many of us went into the Invader directly from pilot training and had never flown anything faster than an AT-6 or bigger than a twin Beech. It was like stepping from a motor-scooter to a Cadillac.' By and large Invader pilots thought of themselves as bomber pilots but were flying an aircraft which had more than its share of fighter characteristics. One could perhaps compare it with the Messerschmitt Me 110 or Mitsubishi G4M, but there really was no other twin with this kind of performance – except, of course, the Mosquito!

Typical of A-26 Invader pilots was Captain Joseph Laurio of the 386th Bomb Group, operating the A-26B from Beaumont-sur-Oise in France in early 1945. 'The A-26 was a quantum leap in high-powered performance over the A-20, with a heavy punch and a lot of staying power. On a typical mission, we would range around 100 miles (161km) behind the front lines searching for targets of opportunity and, of course, dodging ground fire that came up at us. On daylight missions you couldn't always see the ground fire, even from a heavy weapon like an 88mm gun, but we somehow learned to sense it. In time, the Germans were reluctant to shoot at us unnecessarily because they knew we'd turn on them.'

'The A-26 Invader', he recalls, 'was a real lady. Treat her right and she'd treat you right. But you had to know what the rudder was for, because the airplane had a very powerful turn when you were on the rudder pedals and a lot of guys let it get away from them. Attacking a ground target in an A-26 with the nose guns blazing, you *knew* you were making trouble for the bad guys.'

Sixty-seven Invaders were lost to all causes in European fighting, but Invaders also totted up a rather remarkable seven confirmed air-to-air kills. Figures for losses in the Pacific theatre were apparently never totted up, but are understood to have been low.

Edward Heinemann, whose name is closely associated with design of both the A-20 and the A-26, has of course become one of aviation's best-known design virtuosos. T. R. Smith, the Douglas project engineer on the A-26, later designed the highly successful Aero Commander series of light twin aircraft. The sole XA-26F (44-34586) was a testbed fitted with a General Electric I-16 jet engine in the rear fuselage. Post-war versions of the Invader included YB-26K, B-26K and A-26A variants modified by On Mark for operations in South-East Asia. The US Navy operated ninety-eight JD-1 (UB-26J) and fifty-two JD-1D (DB-26J) Invaders, the former as target tugs and the latter as drone controller aircraft.

Although the post-war role of American bombers lies outside the scope of this volume, special mention should be made of the durability of the A-26 Invader and of the fact that transport conversions abounded in the 1950s, at a time before executive transports were designed as such from the outset. Redesignated B-26 (after the B-26 Marauder was no longer in service), the Invader fought valiantly in Korea where one pilot earned a Medal of Honor. And, elsewhere, the Invader fought in Algeria, Cuba, Indo-China and Vietnam. As late as 1969 Invaders were not merely being used but being used in combat – in South-East Asia – a record of longevity almost unmatched in aviation history.

'For some reason, good photos of the A-26 Invader taken during World War II are difficult to find,' says Harry Gann of Douglas Aircraft. Thanks to Mr Gann, this view, released on 1 February 1945, shows A-26B Invader 41-39186 of the Ninth Air Force in flight during the final days of the conflict. The dorsal turret was governed to prevent zealous airmen from shooting the bomber's tail off. (Douglas)

# B-26 Marauder

The Martin B-26 Marauder was one of the sleekest and most beautiful flying machines ever built. Near the end of the war on 30 January 1945, while an attendant worker with fire bottle watches at Middle River Airport, a pilot prepares to crank up B-26G-25-MA Marauder 44-68144, apparently on a delivery flight. (Martin)

In the late 1930s and early 1940s a few thinkers in the United States – Alexander de Seversky among them – predicted that airpower would win (or lose) future wars and that other methods of fighting would be relegated to secondary importance. These men foresaw giant bombers spanning oceans to bring the war home with devastating finality to an enemy, who was usually portrayed as some sort of bug-eyed, buck-toothed foreign fellow unable to build giant bombers of his own.

These ideas were popular among the followers of US Army Air Corps Brigadier General William (Billy) Mitchell who predicted an air attack on Hawaii, proved that aeroplanes could obliterate battleships, and was court-martialled and cashiered for being a decade and a half ahead of his time. Aeroplanes *did* attack Pearl Harbor and sank the dreadnoughts *Repulse* and *Prince of Wales* in the first days of the Pacific war, and ultimately long-range bombers brought Japan to its knees without an armed invasion of the Japanese home islands. But the

With apparent French hedgerows passing underneath, Martin B-26 Marauders in camouflage warpaint press onward. The Marauder was not initially liked by combat air crews in the ETO (European Theatre of Operations) and in the early days of bombing missions losses were higher than they should have been. In time, however, the Marauder acquired an enviable record. (USAF)

Women Air Service Pilots (WASPs) served in segregated units and were not permitted to fly in combat, but they made an enormous contribution ferrying bombers across oceans to the bomb groups overseas. These WASP members are walking in front of a row of Marauders at Laredo Army Air Base, Texas, circa 1943. While they may be B-26s, these Laredo-based aeroplanes are more likely to be Martin AT-23 Marauder advanced trainers. (via Dave Ostrowski)

advocates of the long-range bomber were not entirely right.

As it turned out, the success against Japan became possible only because ground and naval forces obtained airfields in the western Pacific at enormous cost in blood and treasure. More importantly, the mighty bombers predicted by the advocates of airpower proved to be only a part of the story. This examination of US bombers in World War II has already demonstrated that, if four-engined long-range aircraft like the Flying Fortress were important, twin-engined machines like the Havoc and Invader also played a role.

John Bull Stirling, a retired US Air Force colonel of Reston, Virginia, is one of those intrepid officers who fought in combat in three wars: he began his career in the Martin B-26 Marauder in the Pacific and ended it in the McDonnell RF-101C Voodoo in Vietnam. Stirling is an advocate for airpower, but hastily acknowledges that footsoldiers and sailors played a vital role in the 1945 victory.

Nothing gets this American pilot more annoyed than the suggestion that the war was won by four-engined bombers. Perhaps thinking of the terrible losses of men and equipment cited in the first chapter, Stirling points out that it took years to get the big bombers designed, developed, and into

combat. 'Even after the "biggies" came along, they were vastly outnumbered by the smaller aircraft which flew the shorter-range missions closer to where the enemy infantryman was shooting at our boys. If you had to pick a single type of machine which really won the war, you'd have to say that World War II was really won by the fast, twin-engined bombers.'

'Of course', he admits, 'no single weapon did it all. But those of us who flew in the Martin B-26 Marauder sometimes felt that we got the short end of the stick when the resources were passed out and the dangers had to be faced. I know about those twelve thousand heavy bombers lost during the war, but has anybody ever tallied up the total number of Marauders, or the total number of medium and light bombers? Some-how I doubt it . . .'

Another B-26 Marauder pilot, Lt.-Col. M. P. Curphey, says that no other aircraft type contributed so much or was so wrongly maligned. 'I know the guys in the heavies suffered terribly on those high-altitude missions over Berlin, but have you ever tried to chase a train over a hedgerow in France at 100 feet [30.48m] of altitude in a twin-engine bomber moving at 400mph [644km/h] while everybody in the world was blasting away at you with 88mm cannon? Don't tell me us Marauder guys didn't do our part!'

Martin B-26C Marauder 41-34678 wearing the early US national insignia of the war period, in the grass at AAF Materiel Command, Wright Field, Ohio in about 1942. Martin later put out a release pointing out that Marauders saw action in the South Pacific, Alaska, Madagascar, North Africa, Italy, France and Germany and that the Marauder had the lowest loss rate in combat of any US aircraft in the European theatre. (via Dave Ostrowski)

## Bad Reputation

'Widowmaker' and 'Flying Coffin' were among nick-names applied to the Martin B-26 Marauder. The Marauder was, plain and simple, an aircraft widely understood to be 'hot', overpowered, and dangerous to fly. It mattered not that the reputation was unfair or that the criticism was often uttered by those who did not know.

The sleek B-26 actually proved dangerous, as it turned out, for its adversaries. Its reputation for being 'too hot to handle' was not exactly undeserved – if the truth were to be told, relatively few aircraft types warrant the soubriquet 'forgiving' – but if the Marauder was not exactly user-friendly in the right

hands it was both effective and formidable. Further-more, it had the bomb load, speed and staying power to make plenty of trouble for the bad guys.

Going back to the pre-war B-10 and earlier, the Glenn L. Martin Company in Baltimore, Maryland, was long recognized as a leading designer and builder of bombers. In 1938 Martin produced its Model 167F bomber which did not win any US orders but was sold to France and later to Britain as the Martin Maryland. Development of the Marauder began when the Martin firm's planners became aware that the US Army Air Corps' Materiel Division at Wright Field, Ohio, had issued Circular Proposal 39-640, dated 11 March 1939.

On 20 April 1944 a B-26 Marauder in natural metal finish with gun packs bristling on its side and post-1943 national insignia, is seen on what appears to be a proving flight near the manufacturer's plant at Middle River, Maryland. Crews found the Marauder roomy and comfortable to work in. Once the aircraft overcame its early reputation, the Marauder was widely appreciated by those who flew it. (via Dave Ostrowski)

Ebel, felt that it could compete effectively. On 5 July 1939 the company submitted a proposal for its Model 179, an aircraft closely resembling the one which was later built except that it had a twin tail.

A single rudder was added to the design by the time the Model 179, now designated B-26 (serial number 40-1361), was rolled out. The B-26 made its first flight on 25 November 1940 with Ebel as pilot and Bob Fenimore and Al Melewski also on board. This first Marauder was not really an experimental prototype but was, in fact, a service aircraft. Pratt & Whitney R-2800-5 Twin Wasp 18-cylinder turbocharged engines delivering 1,850hp drove four-bladed propellers and made possible a top speed, it was claimed, of 392mph, or faster than most fighters then in operational service in the world. The engines were in streamlined nacelles underslung from a shoulder-mounted wing which, over the service life of the B-26, had to be increased in size.

The 'Flying Torpedo' as some called the B-26 Marauder because of its fuselage shape was, in fact, a class act, a silvery sleek bullet of a medium bomber which could tote a respectable bomb load and outrun the opposition. The aeroplane had genuine aesthetic qualities. True, the Marauder landed at around 130mph (209km/h) and it could easily get away from an unskilled pilot. But when figures were added up at the end of the war for the 5,157 Marauders built, the B-26 turned out to have a remarkably safe flying record.

Initially the Marauder's crew totalled seven: pilot, co-pilot, bombardier, navigator, radio-operator/engineer, camera operator and tail gunner. In practice, the number was often six and at times reduced to five. Early aircraft, including the initial batch of 201 machines (serials 40-1361/1561), had a wing span of 65ft (19.12m). Gross weight was around 27,200lb (12,337kg). The maximum bomb load of 5,800lb (2,861kg) proved well in excess of the Army's original proposal.

Most of the initial batch of 201 Marauders were retained for training and experimental purposes. Training proved to be very important since bomber crews of the period were unfamiliar with tricycle landing gear aircraft and were even less well equipped to deal with the Marauder's 'hot' characteristics and high landing speed.

The loss of one Marauder during an early training mission was described by a witness who managed to confuse his metaphors while giving a vivid, contemporaneous account. 'The guy came in on final [approach for landing] like a bat out of hell. He was the same guy who'd been pointing out the day before that the Marauder *landed* as fast as some of the prewar bombers *cruised*. This guy had one wing just a

The proposal was for a new medium bomber, one which would fall between the classes represented by the A-20 Havoc and B-17 Fortress. The new aircraft would require high speed, long range, and a bomb load of 2,000lb (907kg); it was recognized that attainment of these specifications would probably result in high wing-loading and therefore a lengthy take-off run and high landing speed.

In the late 1930s the American medium bomber force was dependent almost entirely on the obsolescent Douglas B-18 Bolo, so the requirement for a new design was, if anything, overdue. Glenn L. Martin's team, headed by designer Peyton M. Magruder and engineer/test-pilot William E. (Ken)

little high and you could see that the bomber was off-kilter when he did exactly the worst thing you could do with a B-26: he arranged it so that the first thing to touch the ground was the nosewheel. Now, you just picture all those tons of bomber all coming down on that spindly little nose landing gear. Anyway, this guy tried to pour on the power to get out of that situation and the left wing hit the ground, crumpled, and exploded. There was a big flash of red-orange fuel fire and suddenly half the aircraft was engulfed in flames. The half we could see broke into pieces and the people came pouring out of it. Incredibly, all of the crew got out of the airplane while it burned itself to a cinder right in front of us – but two of them died before the day was over.'

Operational deliveries to the US Army Air Forces began in 1941 and production soon shifted in that year to the B-26A. Thirty B-26As (41-7345/7365, 41-7368, 41-7431, 41-7477/7483) were built and also introduced self-sealing fuel tanks, two extra ferry tanks in the rear bomb bay, and 555lb (252kg) of armour plate. A further 109 B-26A-1s (41-7366/7367, 41-7369/7430, 41-7432/7476) introduced provision for optional bomb bay fuel tanks, shackles for a 22in (55.88cm) torpedo under the fuselage and 0.50in (12.7mm) machine-guns in lieu of earlier 0.30in (7.62mm) guns. With the B-26A-1, ferry range was increased to 2,600 miles (4,184km).

## To the War Zone

It was with B-26A and B-26A-1 Marauders that the 22nd Bomb Group moved to Australia following the 7 December 1941 Japanese attack on Pearl Harbor. Stationed earlier at Langley Field near Hampton, Virginia, the group had had painful teething pro-blems with the Marauder. At one point some 44 of the 66 aircraft then built were held in storage pending alterations to the nose wheel gear, the design of which was at first too weak for the Marauder's hard landings. For a time, too, no machine-guns were available to arm Marauders coming off the factory line and, to get them to the 22nd Group in time, the manufacturer had to ballast the aircraft with tools and spare parts. The second unit to receive Marauders from the Baltimore production line, the 42nd Bomb Group at Boise, Idaho, was simply unable to become fully opera-tional on the type in time to deploy to the Pacific as planned; added to which, the 42nd lost several aircraft in the all-too-familiar landing accidents.

In April 1942, with some trade-off of extra fuel in exchange for reduced bomb load, the 22nd Bomb Group began bombing targets in New Guinea. Tropical conditions and foul weather were especially

difficult on aeroplanes and crew, and inflicted at least as much harm as the Japanese. B-26A and B-26A-1 Marauders also went quickly to war in the Aleutians.

Four Marauders had been detached from the 22nd Bomb Group en route to Australia and were held at Hickam Field, Hawaii, for training with the torpedo capability that had been belatedly built into the aircraft. As one of the critical battles in the Pacific theatre began to take shape, the four B-26As were shifted to Midway in the hope that they would be effective against Admiral Yamamoto's warships. On 4 June 1942 the four Marauders sighted enemy aircraft-carriers and attacked them at wavecap level, charging through a screen of Zero fighters. Later, the B-26As attacked the carrier *Ryuyo*. The results of these engagements were inconclusive, but they marked a high-water point for the Marauder in the Pacific.

Why was the Marauder less than fully successful in the Pacific, when the North American B-25 Mitchell achieved so much in that vast expanse of ocean? After Midway, it was decided to concentrate Marauders on the other side of the world. The reason seems to have been that rugged individualists in the very difficult operating conditions in the Pacific found the Mitchell to their liking and simply had no reason to press on with a type which was, in the event, available to them only in relatively small numbers.

Continuing to practise torpedo-bombing, the 38th Bomb Group moved on to Australia and operated Marauders in two of its four squadrons before converting to the seemingly preferable B-25 Mitchell. Meanwhile, the 42nd Group, which also developed a capability for torpedo as well as conventional bombing, moved from Idaho to Elmendorf, Alaska. Results were at best inconclusive once again, even as the B-25 was reaching Alaska- and Aleutian-based operators. For the remainder of the conflict the B-25 was far more important than the Marauder in that area.

## B-26B Version

In May 1942 the B-26B version of the Marauder began to come from Martin's production lines. This became the most numerous version of the Marauder with 1,883 examples built. The Glenn L. Martin plant was really getting revved up and was one of the first to employ women on a regular basis, the well-known 'Rosie the Riveter' ladies who kept up the war effort on the home front. With the B-26B-1 variant came an improved engine cowling shape (as a result of which the propeller spinners were deleted), still heavier armour plating, a ventral gun position, and

Martin B-26B Marauder
41-17704 flies through
American skies in 1942,
perhaps preparing to head
overseas and into the fight.
Medium bombers like the
B-26 rarely received the
press attention or the acclaim
of the four-engined
Fortresses and Liberators,
but their impact was felt by
the Axis powers and their
successful bombing missions
were often of more direct
help to the foot soldier at the
front lines. (USAF)

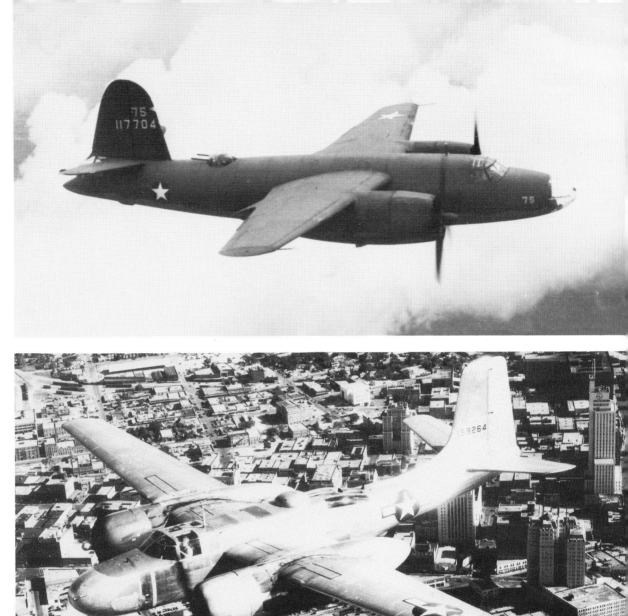

The B-26 Marauder was often
compared with the A-26
Invader (above) even though
the former was a medium
bomber, the latter an attack
aircraft. After VJ-Day, the US
Air Force confused
everybody by redesignating
the Invader as the B-26, only
to return to the original A-26
designation during the
Vietnam era. A-26 Invader
41-39264 is seen over Los
Angeles. (via Dave
Ostrowski)

Martin B-26C Marauder
41-31853 'Lois Rose' of the
455th Bomb Squadron, 323rd
Bomb Group, flew 158
combat missions before being
shot down on 26 December
1944. In its parking spot at a
British airfield, painted with
late markings and 'YU-O'
code, 'Lois Rose' has
tarpaulins over her guns but
appears otherwise ready for
another mission. (via Robert
F. Dorr)

Two views of a Marauder
crew member relaxing on
his aircraft. Martin B-26C
41-34955 'Mission Belle' of
the 455th Bomb Squadron,
323rd Bomb Group, is
covered with marks from her
many bombing missions.
Attitudes about taking
pictures varied from one
bomb group to the next and
the 323rd seems to have
been tolerant. (via Robert F.
Dorr)

Nose close-up of a B-26C
Marauder nicknamed 'Bat-
outa-hell II' of the 323rd
Bomb Group. Names of flight
crew appear beneath pilot's
window. The inscription
further back, in larger letters,
states that the bomber is
maintained by 'Bullet
Turnbull, Ace Engineer' and
a second nickname, 'Putt Putt
Lyon', also appears. (via
Robert F. Dorr)

a second 0.50in (12.7mm) machine-gun in the tail position. With these modifications the Marauder now weighed no less than 36,500lb (16,556kg). Because of the increased weight, the B-26B-2, -3, and -4 required upgraded R-2800-41 or -43 engines which provided 1,920hp each. The B-26B-4 aircraft introduced a lengthened nosewheel strut as a means of increasing the wing's angle of attack on take-off.

The B-26B was known in Britain as the Marauder I. With the B-26B-10 version, an increase in fin and rudder area earned the aircraft the less formal appellation 'big-assed bird'. Next came the B-26B-20 variants in which the hand-held 0.50in (12.7mm) guns in the tail were replaced by a Martin-Bell turret that electro-hydraulically operated the two guns. Because the tail gun position was now shortened, the fuselage length of this Marauder dropped from 58ft 3in (17.75m) to 56ft 1in (17.09m). The tail gunner enjoyed better protection from thicker glass and an armoured bulkhead.

Sitting in the tail of the Marauder was not, as might be imagined, any easy task. To be sure, Marauders usually operated at lower altitude than the heavy bombers, so a man had less chance of freezing or of having his skin come off when in direct contact with bitter-cold metal. But as Staff Sergeant Arthur Khiem remembers, the job was a challenge. 'The Marauder was a highly manoeuvr-able aircraft as well as a fast one, and when you were strapped in behind the tail gun, you kept getting thrown from side to side – like being in the caboose of a train going around sharp curves. Moving to or from the gunner's seat was so difficult that once you got settled in place, you usually stayed there for the entire mission. Visibility was okay but not great. And of course while everybody else knew where you were going, the guy in back knew only where you'd been. Handling the guns was difficult, spotting an enemy fighter against the fast-receding ground was difficult, in fact the whole thing was difficult.'

Other minor changes were introduced into sub-variants, including the B-26B-30, given the British name Marauder II. All one hundred aircraft in this series were delivered to the South African Air Force. By the end of the B-26B production run, standard US Army khaki camouflage was viewed as unnecessary and Marauders, like many other US bomber types, were beginning to be delivered in their natural metal finish. With its torpedo-shaped fuselage and rakish, powerful appearance, the Marauder looked even more impressive in unpainted silver and the deletion of colour may have added a few miles per hour to its airspeed. One of the bomb groups flying these B-26 Marauders adopted the nickname (borrowed from Eastern Air Lines) 'The Great Silver Fleet'.

Beating up an airfield at low altitude was easier to do during World War II than in the more restrictive environment of today. This natural-metal B-26 Marauder is making its presence felt. (Martin)

The 319th Bomb Group at Barksdale Field in Bossier City, Lousiana, began working up with newly delivered Marauder bombers in June 1942 (concurrent with the 320th Group at MacDill Field near Tampa, Florida). As planned, the 319th moved to England and thence to North Africa, beginning on 21 September 1942, but this combat deployment was something of a fiasco. Of fifty-seven aircraft with which the group began stateside operations, only thirty-four reached Norfolk, England, for onward shipment to Tafaroui, Algeria, and just half of these, seventeen B-26s, reached Algeria by 21 November 1942. In its first 21 days of combat operations, the 319th Group flew an unimpressive ten bombing missions and lost ten aircraft. Much of this was due to the appalling conditions under which US combat airmen had to labour in their early days in this theatre, but the poor luck of the 319th did not help the Marauder's reputation.

## Combat in Europe

When the B-26 Marauder first went to war in Europe, operations by the 322nd Bomb Group were far from successful. On 17 May 1943 a mission by ten Marauders headed by Colonel Robert M. Stillman resulted in what may have been the most disastrous mission in history – a 100 per cent loss of all Marauders to anti-aircraft fire, Luftwaffe fighters and mid-air collision. Only two men survived to return to the devastated bomb group.

This was the second Marauder mission in Europe and, for a time, the last. Lieutenant General Ira C. Eaker decided that, for the present at least, the Martin medium bomber could add little to the war

effort already being mounted by the four-engined B-17 and B-24. There were various frustrations 'setting up' with the B-26, in part because for a time the type equipped only one squadron of one group, but none of the difficulties seems to have been attributable to any basic flaw in the bomber itself. Under the Ninth Air Force formed at the end of 1943 in anticipation of the invasion of Europe, the Marauder was far more successful than with Eaker's Eighth.

## C Model Marauder

Externally identical to the B-26B, the B-26C was a product of the Omaha, Nebraska, factory which Martin occupied for the purpose of manufacturing Marauders. They called Omaha a 'cowtown', out there in the centre of the country far from the excitement of either coast, but it was a young city of straight and sturdy people and on the aircraft production line some of them set new records. Here, too, 'Rosie the Riveter' went to work. The distinctive roar of Pratt & Whitney R-2800 engines and the silhouettes of low-level Marauders over the flat Nebraska expanses quickly became routine.

Orders placed as early as 1941 called for 1,200 aircraft in the B-26C series, followed by a further batch of 385, after which the Omaha plant switched to production of the B-29 Superfortress. Included in the B-26C series were some 194 aircraft which went to the US Navy under the designation JM-1 and were used for target-towing and other non-combatant duties. A few of the Navy aircraft were fitted with cameras for the reconnaissance role and were designated JM-1.

The designation B-26D was applied to a single Marauder modified early in the war to test hot-air

Throughout the war the authorities vacillated between camouflaging aircraft to make them harder for the enemy to see and brightening-up aircraft to allow 'friendlies' to see them better. The invasion stripes worn by Marauders and other warplanes during the Normandy landings on 6 June 1944 were an example of the latter arrangement. B-26C Marauder 42-107692 belongs to the 323rd Bomb Group. (via Robert F. Dorr)

de-icing of the wing and tail leading edges. Testing of various de-icing methods was *de rigeur* throughout the war.

The B-26E was a proposal for a much lightened version of the B-26B with the dorsal turret moved forward to the navigator's compartment and the weight reduced to around 31,000lb (14,061kg). The concept was not pursued and most sources on the Marauder indicate that no B-26E was actually built. It would appear, contrary to conventional wisdom, that there was a sole B-26E – itself a converted 'B' model (41-34680) – nicknamed 'Gypsy Rose' and that it was used for development work, with a few of its features actually being adopted on later Marauders.

Production of the B-26F Marauder began in late 1943, with initial deliveries occurring in February 1944. This version had the wider-span wings but the wing incidence was increased by 3.5deg to improve take-off and landing characteristics. This variant had no fixed nose gun in the bombardier's compartment and the torpedo rack on the fuselage keel was deleted. About 200 of these went to the RAF, which passed most of them on to the South African Air Force; with British equipment installed, it was designated Marauder III.

The B-26G Marauder was identified by numerous minor changes in equipment and fittings. Of 893 built, some 150 were acquired by the RAF and were also known as the Marauder III. Fifty-seven TB-26G trainer aircraft were built in 1944, and thirty-two of these went to the US Navy and Marine Corps in March 1945 as the JM-2. A B-26G was the final Marauder off the production line and flew on 18 April 1945.

## Marauder Performance

Performance figures for World War II aircraft always arouse debate. It is not unusual to hear a former crewman speaking of the Marauder burning through the air at some 400mph (644km/h) and leaving Messerschmitts and Mitsubishis struggling in its wake when, in fact, although very fast, the B-26 attained no such speed.

Was the Marauder, as its advocates claim, the fastest medium bomber of the war? Company figures show the B-26B variant as capable of 298mph (480km/h) at 15,000ft (4,572m) and give the bomber's cruising speed as 294mph (473km/h) at 15,000ft (4,572m). These figures demonstrate how numbers can be vexing. Since individual aircraft performed differently on different days and one Marauder was slightly different from another – to say nothing of various conditions such as wind, temperature, etc – is there really any meaning to a statement about flying speed which draws a distinction of 4mph (6.4km/h) between cruise and maximum? Furthermore, are these figures not significantly lower than actual speeds reached by Marauders in the combat zone?

The same company figures tell us that the B-26G version had a maximum speed of 274mph (441km/h) at 15,000ft (4,572m). Figures credit the Marauder with an initial rate of climb of 1,300ft/min (6.6m/sec) and a service ceiling above 15,000ft (4,572m). The latter version was said to have a range of 675 miles (1,086km) while carrying a realistic bomb load of 4,000lb (1,815kg). Without a belly full of bombs, the Marauder had a maximum ferry range of 1,875 miles (3,017km).

Final view from 323rd Bomb Group camera buff shows B-26C Marauder 41-18289 with work being performed during a lull in European fighting. The starboard engine cowling has been removed by hard-working maintenance men and a scaffold has been set up to serve the port engine as well. (via Robert F. Dorr)

The 'short-wing' Marauders (up through B-26B-4) had a wing span of 65ft (19.81m), while later machines (from B-26B-5) spanned 71ft (21.64m). Wing area on early machines was 602sq ft (55.93m²) and on later Marauders became 658sq ft (61.13m²). Length of the Marauder varied, the original B-26 being 56ft (17.07m) long while the B-26A, 'B and 'C measured 58ft 3in (17.75m) and the B-26F and 'G were 56ft 1in (17.09m) in length. Height was 19ft 10in (6.04m) for those aeroplanes up through the B-26C, and 20ft 4in (6.19m) for all later machines. The undercarriage track of the Marauder was the same for all models, namely 21ft 11¼in (6.68m).

From these figures it will be apparent that, although many suspected it was bigger, the B-26 Marauder was in fact just about the same size as the B-25 Mitchell. The Douglas A-26 Invader, which came later in the war, was comparable in size but was not classified as a medium bomber because, by then, definitions of size had changed.

Early versions of the Marauder had an empty weight of around 25,500lb (11,569kg) and a fully loaded weight of 35,000lb (15,876kg). A typical B-26G Marauder had an empty weight of 25,500lb (11,569kg) and a maximum all-up weight of 38,200lb (17,328kg).

Armament consisted of one flexible and one fixed forward-firing gun in the nose with 270 and 200 rounds respectively, two 'package' guns on each side of the forward lower fuselage in fixed forward-firing position with 200–250 rounds per gun, two guns in the dorsal power turret with 400 rounds apiece, two guns in the power mount in the tail with 800–900 rounds per gun, and two flexibly mounted guns in the after fuselage with 240–250 rounds each; all these weapons were 0.50in (12.7mm) Colt Browning machine-guns. The Marauder's main bomb bay could accommodate two 2,000lb (907kg) or 1,600lb (726kg) bombs or four 1,000lb (454kg) bombs. Other bomb loads could include six 500lb (227kg) or ten 250lb (113kg) or twenty 150lb (68kg) bombs. All early versions of the Marauder (through B-26C), as has been noted, were equipped to carry a 2,000lb (907kg) torpedo on the centre-line.

Reference has already been made to the use of the Marauder by the RAF. In July 1942 the RAF's No 14 Squadron in Egypt began replacing its Bristol Blenheims with the Marauder I, which was identical to the B-26A variant with the smaller 65ft (19.81m) wing span. Just as the Marauder was regarded as 'hot' and 'tricky' elsewhere, in the RAF it was subjected to critical scrutiny and further deliveries were delayed. No 14 remained for a long period the only squadron equipped with the type.

The South African Air Force's Marauder IIs went to Nos 12, 21, 24, 25 and 30 Squadrons, operating in North Africa. In 1944 a batch of Marauder IIIs (B-26F and B-26G models) arrived in the Mediterranean theatre to become a part of the South Africans' efforts. Marauders subsequently served with the French Air Force, equipping the 31e and 34e Escadres (31st and 34th Wings) with three squadrons each. The French took first delivery in September 1943 and eventually had on charge some 150 B-26C and B-26G aircraft. Lend-Lease records show that 525 Marauders of all variants went to Britain.

Outwardly indistinguishable from the B-26 medium bomber, the AT-23 was delivered to the USAAF to train crews who would then go into combat in the bomber version. Martin AT-23B Marauder 41-35872 at Laredo airfield, Texas. (USAF)

From almost any angle the Martin B-26 Marauder was a graceful and beautiful aircraft. This frontal view taken by the manufacturer has little to disclose about the markings and insignia on the aircraft, but shows what it looked like to have the Marauder coming straight at you. (Martin)

No list of B-26 Marauders would be complete without mention of the US Army Air Forces' following the usual pattern of developing a trainer version under a separate designation. In the case of the Marauder, 208 aircraft were ordered as the AT-23A advanced trainer, beginning in 1941. These were stripped of armament and other combat equipment and were used, not for training, but as target tugs.

A second batch of 375 trainers was produced as the AT-23B. These also had combat equipment deleted and were employed as target tugs, some 324 of them reaching the US Navy as JM-1s.

A further development by the Martin company, which it is appropriate to mention here, was the twin-engined XB-27 bomber.

Before the war Martin had worked on a design to meet Air Corps specification XC-214 for a high-altitude medium bomber. The aircraft would have been similarly powered to the B-26 Marauder, its engines being two 2,100hp Pratt & Whitney R-2800-9 Double Wasps. With a seven-man crew, the aircraft would have had a wing span of 84ft (25.60m), an empty weight of 23,125lb (10,489kg) and a gross weight of 32,970lb (14,954kg). The designation XB-27 was assigned early in development work.

Judging from the little information about the XB-27 that has survived, there appears to have been no particular flaw in the basic design of the aircraft. So many little-known aircraft were in the design stages during the war that the reason for choosing one type over another often remains obscure. Apparently, because there were other twin-engined bombers which came close to the specified performance –

among them the B-25 Mitchell and B-26 Marauder – development of the XB-27 was not proceeded with and the aircraft was not built.

## Combat Saga

Despite the initial difficulties and the disastrous 'hundred per cent loss' mission in Europe, the B-26 Marauder became extremely effective in combat and was well liked by crews. On 26 March 1944 Marauders of the 322nd Bomb Group exacted a kind of retaliation against the Reich for the earlier losses, when 54 Marauders led a 344-bomber strike on E-boat facilities at the location of the earlier debacle, Ijmuiden, Holland, unloading some 100 tons of bombs. On this mission, no Marauders were lost in combat, although twenty aircraft returned to base suffering battle damage.

As the Marauder became accepted, crews were retrained for medium-altitude missions using the magnificent Norden bomb sight, which was itself one of the miracles of the war. Following their successful role in covering the 6 June 1944 invasion of Normandy, Marauders proved successful in attacking German V-1 flying-bomb launching sites. The latter missions were code-named 'Noball' and became increasingly important in 1944 as the 'doodle-bugs' began to fall on England.

The Marauder's 'Widowmaker' reputation persisted – undeservedly – and a few grumbled about some of the type's shortcomings, including chronic leaks in the hydraulic system, which was prone not merely to leak but to take damage from ground fire. Maintenance men were quick to assert that the B-26 was far from the easiest aeroplane to keep in

good order, especially when operations shifted to less prepared airfields on the European continent. The difficulties with the nose gear of the Marauder were never fully resolved. Still, the Martin bombers demonstrated a high sortie rate and gained an impressive reputation for precision attacks on road, rail and other transport targets in Europe.

As the fighting in Europe drew to its conclusion, a fair number of B-26s achieved the difficult task of completing fully 100 combat missions. Three hundred and fifty Marauders are reputed to have reached this figure and one machine, nicknamed 'Flak Bait', finished 202 combat sorties. Now dismembered with its nose on display in Washington, DC's National Air and Space Museum, 'Flak Bait' is reputedly the only surviving Marauder that saw a lengthy period of combat.

One of the reasons why so few examples of the Marauder survived is that in the immediate post-victory period in Europe, no effort was made to return surplus B-26s to the US while hundreds were broken up for scrap on German soil. Likewise, at domestic US bases, B-26s and AT-23s were scrapped en masse in about 1946 – a time when no one was thinking about saving or salvaging airframes for any purpose. Says one officer, 'It was not picked as one of the types to continue in service. I remember a post-war news reel showing how they would set off a charge – apparently right at the main spar and fuselage juncture – and blow up the airplane, and then a bulldozer would come along and finish the job.' Another remembers surviving aircraft in the Pacific being flown to Biak Island where they were blown up in a mass aircraft 'graveyard'. Two Marauders in France received civil registrations while being employed as test-beds for the SNECMA Atar 101 turbojet engine, and among the few survivors some served as executive transports in the US in the 1950s.

## Marauder Users

Bomb Groups of the USAAF that were equipped with the B-26 Marauder included the 4th, 22nd, 42nd, 335th, and 336th within the continental US. In the Mediterranean theatre, the 17th, 319th, and 320th Bomb Groups had the twin-engined Martin aircraft on charge. In Europe, Marauder units were the 322nd, 323rd, 344th, 386th, 387th, 391st, 394th, and 397th Bomb Groups. The Pacific units employing the B-26 were the 22nd and 38th Bomb Groups.

It should be noted that although the Marauder was never intended as a fighter, its pilots were not reluctant to attack the enemy's flying machines. In fact, the B-26 Marauder achieved a number of air-

to-air victories, notably against the giant Messerschmitt Me 323 transport. In North Africa, Marauders shot down a number of other transport types such as the SIAI-Marchetti S.82, Junkers Ju 52, and Junkers Ju 90. On at least one occasion, a Marauder even shot down a Messerschmitt Bf 109!

## Stump Jumper

To conclude the roster of designations applied to Marauder variants, it should be noted that the term XB-26H was given to a single machine (55-68221, a former B-26G) which was converted to test 'bicycle' tandem-wheel landing gear. The purpose was to evaluate the landing gear arrangement later adopted for the Boeing XB-47 and Martin XB-48 post-war jet bombers. The sole XB-26H, because of its ungainly appearance, was nicknamed the 'Middle River Stump Jumper', Middle River being the name of the Baltimore Airport where the Martin firm had its headquarters. With this under-carriage, the XB-26H had its engines canted upward at 3.5deg and outrigger 'training wheels' fitted beneath the engine nacelles.

Not many aeroplanes conclude their life's story within a single decade, but the powerful and graceful Martin Marauder did exactly that. Not yet a fleshed-out design concept in 1939, the Marauder had all but disappeared from the world's skies by 1949, all 5,000 examples having been lost, scrapped, or set aside in the nooks and crannies from which a few preserved examples would later emerge. There simply was no place for the Marauder in the post-war US air arm and no effort was made to identify a role for it.

AiResearch Aviation Company, a subsidiary of Garrett, did the financially attractive refurbishing which turned a few Marauders into executive transports and kept a handful flying in this capacity until 1965. The few pampered businessmen who went on their travels had luxury, comfort, and picture windows, there being two passenger compartments sumptuously arranged for six and ten people respectively. It may have been fine for the participants, but it seemed an undignified conclusion for a maligned medium bomber that had proved itself again and again in determining the outcome of the war.

'The guys who flew it thought it was a wonderful airplane,' says Lt. Col. R. J. Mills, who remembers that Lyndon B. Johnson received the Silver Star award for a mission in the B-26 in New Guinea. Mills points out that – reputation aside – the Marauder had fewer losses per sorties flown than any of the other medium bomber types. 'It seems a pity that less than a half-dozen Marauders survive today.'

Adds Mills, 'If I think about the war on the Western Front after the [Normandy] invasion, I think not about the heavy bombers but about the mediums. They were great tactical airplanes when you needed more than a fighter. You get an airplane like the Marauder, it could be used in either a tactical mode or a strategic mode, depending on what job needed to be done. The mediums were all assigned to the Tactical Air Forces in Europe but sometimes it's hard to draw a line on jobs. The mediums

had to fly the same kind of mission as the often heavies.'

Likewise, Johnson aside, the Marauder seems a remarkably anonymous aeroplane. If the Mitchell had its 'Pappy' Gunn, the Superfortress its Curtis LeMay, the Marauder seems to be associated with no person in particular who flew it to glory. The B-26 fought admirably at the behest of ordinary men who gave it their best and won the war without ever attaining personal glory.

Two views of Martin XB-26H Marauder 44-68221, given the nickname 'Middle River Stump Jumper', which was used to test tandem or 'bicycle' landing gear for the XB-47 and XB-48 jet bombers. Converted from the last B-26G built, this aircraft assisted development of a post-war generation of jet bombers. (Martin)

# B-24 Liberator

The classic outlines of the Consolidated Liberator, including its thin Davis wing and nose gun turret, show up well in this view of Ford-built B-24H 42-7718. Given the clean separation of the paint scheme and the absence of scratches, dents or unit markings, this B-24H is almost certainly on an early proving flight near the Willow Run factory. (USAF)

With just one exception the Consolidated B-24 was the most numerous American aircraft ever built. Compared with the 7,377 Lancasters and 12,731 Flying Fortresses which poured at incredible speed from the jaws of the Western industrial machine, no fewer than 18,325 Liberators were built. This figure also exceeds production totals for Dakotas, Mustangs, Thunderbolts, Mitchells and Marauders. In fact, the number went to 19,023, with spares and related transport variants.

The American capacity to produce Liberators seemed to have no limit. Liberators rolled off production lines belonging to Consolidated, Douglas (at Tulsa, Oklahoma), Ford (at Willow Run, Michigan) and North American (at Dallas).

At one base in the south-west, for a time, Liberators were parked wingtip-to-wingtip as far as the eye could see, stretching off the end of the airfield and out into the desert. 'We were building them faster than we could muster the pilots to fly them overseas,' a veteran remembers. 'You could look out, and there was no end to the sight of Liberators heading toward the horizon.'

Quantity was the major American contribution to the war effort: the great industrial giant created aircraft in numbers that were almost stupefying.

But quantity was not everything. It was not true that the Liberator was viewed as 'second best', a kind of inferior partner to the Fortress. Without even mentioning its revolutionary Davis wing (see later), the Liberator was in every respect the product of an engineering team which sought the very best and came close to achieving it. A widely held notion that the B-24 was somehow poorly constructed, or less widely used, or made less of a contribution, is just plain wrong.

Merely to use one means of measurement, namely the number of squadrons which flew the aircraft into battle, Allan G. Blue, leading historian on the Liberator, has figures which show that the Liberator was no second cousin: the Liberator was original equipment for nineteen bomb groups in Europe and fifteen in the Mediterranean, the total of 34 exceeding by seven the number of bomb groups that were sent into European combat in the Fortress.

Blue's figures show that these Liberator groups flew 226,775 sorties and unloaded 452,508 tons of bombs to hasten the defeat of the Reich.

The plentiful B-24 Liberator served in every theatre. Images of the Liberator making a low-level raid on the Nazi oilfields in Ploesti, Rumania, are unforgettable, but the Liberator must also be remembered for daring long-range solo missions in the vast stretches of the Pacific and for accompanying the B-17 Fortress into Hitler's Fortress Europe.

An exceedingly potent bomber with an innovative wing designed for long range, the Liberator somehow managed to make its imprint on history without ever evoking the love felt by pilots towards the better-publicized B-17 – 'some loved the Lib, some hated it,' says one – and the Liberator was far from fault-free. Still, by virtue of sheer numbers, it could be argued that the B-24 Liberator was the most important US bomber of them all. (The only American aircraft produced in greater numbers is the latter-day Bell UH-1 Huey helicopter in all its civil and military versions.)

If strengths and weaknesses are to be recited, the Liberator owed strength and success to a unique wing planform sold to Consolidated in 1937 by a near-destitute inventor, David R. Davis, who owned the patent and had little else to offer. Although the president of Consolidated, Reuben H. Fleet, and others were sceptical, wind-tunnel tests showed Davis's family of wing sections to give greater performance than any aerofoils then in use. Results showed that the 'remarkably high value for the Davis wing is probably associated with a peculiar variation of boundary layer thickness with angle of attack'; the wing was first employed, and proved itself, on a company flying-boat, the Model 31. Basically, it was a slender wing with sharp camber and a reflex curve on the underside. On the Liberator, it provided superb lift to an ungraceful and ungainly bomber.

If a weakness must be cited to put the B-24 Liberator in perspective, the fault would lie with the hydraulically operated ailerons, flaps and other controls on the bomber. The hydraulics dripped, leading to the joke that the Liberator had been designed as a flying-boat but leaked so badly they put wheels on it. Hydraulics and the oxygen system

were highly vulnerable. 'The aircraft could become an acetylene torch,' says Chuck Williams, who flew with the 460th Bomb Group from Spinazola, Italy. The B-17 Fortress lacked this flaw because its controls were electrical, but even Williams – no apologist for the plane he flew – stakes the claim that the Liberator went 'higher, farther and faster than the B-17'.

## Gear Trouble

The B-24 Liberator suffered from other problems. As with the Martin Marauder (previous chapter), its undercarriage was a source of worry. To the flight engineer or some other enlisted crew member fell the hapless task of peering out of the waist window to see whether the landing gear was down and secured. Too often it was not.

Williams: 'There was a little red knuckle that was supposed to slide into place to fix the gear in the down and locked position. If the weather was poor or the lighting was bad, you couldn't tell whether that knuckle was in place or not. And it had a tendency not to be, which is why you've seen so many instances of B-24s with collapsed landing gear even when they suffered no battle damage. We loved that airplane and we hated it.'

A love-hate relationship it may have been, but in the planning rooms of Berlin and Tokyo, there was never a moment's doubt that the Liberator was a very formidable American weapon of war.

The prototype XB-24 aircraft (39-556), known to its manufacturer as the Consolidated Model 32, shined in natural metal and seemed virginal with its plain markings when it went aloft at San Diego on 29 December 1939 with William B. Wheatley at the controls.

Wheatley was a no-nonsense pragmatist who wore a railroad engineer's work cap as a trademark and he kept his enthusiasm for the new aircraft behind a guarded exterior. The prototype had no turbo-super-chargers on its Pratt & Whitney R-1830 Twin Wasp 14-cylinder engines and was armed with but six 0.50in (12.7mm) guns in single mounts. Like the Catalina and Coronado flying-boats being turned out by the company, the XB-24 was big but not breathtaking.

The basic Liberator design owed more, perhaps, to pragmatism than to beauty. It was impressive but not graceful, with a deep and stumpy fuselage, its thin metal skin surrounding a pair of bomb bays which could each carry 4,000lb (1,814kg) of bombs, with a catwalk down the centre for structural bracing and to enable the crew to move between front and back.

The beginning. On 28 January 1940, just a month after its first flight, the prototype XB-24, or Consolidated Model 32 (39-680) flies over the California desert near San Diego. This first Liberator was rudimentary but the configuration was established and during the war years Liberators were to come off factory lines in astronomical numbers. (Consolidated)

On another test flight on 13 July 1941, the first XB-24 Liberator (39-680) flies through clouds near San Diego. (via R. J. Mills, Jr)

Ahead of American Liberators on the San Diego production line, the Liberator II for the RAF was the first operational variant of the famous Consolidated bomber. This aircraft, wearing British roundels, is making a pre-delivery flight over California on 29 October 1941. (via R. J. Mills, Jr)

Changes in the Liberator's configuration are evident in these views of aircraft built by Consolidated in San Diego. B-24D 42-40092, wearing the camouflage discarded later in the war, has a solid nose armed with swivel-mounted machine-guns and pre-1943 US national insignia. B-24J 44-40071, also seen at San Diego's Lindbergh Field, has an Emerson turret in the nose, natural metal finish, and the national emblem adopted by the US later in the war. (via Dave Ostrowski)

The Liberator was entered by flicking a small hydraulic lever on the right side of the bomb bay. The bomb bay doors folded into themselves like a roll-top desk and the crew climbed up on the catwalk.

The original crew of seven grew to eleven as the Liberator was developed during the war years. On a typical mission, the Liberator was manned by pilot, co-pilot, navigator, bombardier, flight engineer/radioman and four or five gunners. Key features of the Liberator design, in addition to the Davis wing, included twelve flexible fuel cells in the wings, a Minneapolis-Honeywell auto-pilot, Fowler flaps, and unusual main undercarriage units comprising single legs curved round the outside of large single wheels which retracted hydraulically outwards to lie flat in the wing, where the wheel projected below the undersurface and needed a fairing.

The new bomber and its Davis wing were unproven and even the idea of a bomber with four engines was far from universally accepted. With Hitler's forces overrunning the Low Countries and the European continent being torn by war – even if Americans did not realize its significance yet – besieged Britain and France did not hesitate to order quantities of the export version. The LB-30 export Liberator came ahead of the US variants and contributed to their development.

The designation was unfortunate. The US Army had a clear enough system for naming its aeroplanes and under this system the term XB-30 was applied to a Lockheed proposal for a bomber that was never built (although the aircraft design was resurrected as the C-69 Constellation and became one of the most graceful transport aeroplanes of all time). 'LB' was a

Consolidated, not Army, abbreviation for Land Bomber. But the LB-30 design preceded the second Liberator, the YB-24 service-test aircraft, which flew on 13 August 1940.

The Consolidated Aircraft Company had recently moved from frigid Buffalo in upstate New York to temperate San Diego in southern California, and conditions were ripe for the firm to become a source of the US Army's second heavy bomber, after the B-17 Fortress. Designer Isaac M. (Mac) Laddon, backed by Fleet, had enormous confidence in the Liberator and never allowed the Army or anyone else to tell him that Consolidated should settle for a secondary role as a second-source producer of the B-17. Instead, Laddon persuaded Army Air Corps chief Major General Henry H. (Hap) Arnold to go with the B-24.

## Modest Prototype

The first aircraft, the XB-24 (39-680), was powered by 1,100hp R-1830-33 engines. In March 1939 the US Army Air Corps ordered seven YB-24s (the 'Y' prefix indicating a service test role). Before further progress could be made, however, the Army ordered a number of changes in the design. The 1,100hp R-1830-33 engines were replaced by 1,200hp R-1830-41s equipped with General Electric B-2 turbo-superchargers instead of mechanical two-speed superchargers, for high-altitude flights.

Originally built with the first 'wet wing' on an American military aircraft, the prototype had to be refitted with self-sealing fuel tanks as well as modified engine controls that permitted as much as 60 per cent power if the controls were shot away. These alterations raised the gross weight of the first

Liberators from 38,300lb (17,432kg) to over 41,000lb (18,600kg). When the changes were made on the XB-24, it was redesignated XB-24B and flew with the latter designation on 1 February 1941.

After the second YB-24 Liberator had been delivered, the remaining six YBs were diverted to the British as LB-30As, together with twenty B-24A production aircraft which went to Britain as the LB-30B.

Production went ahead of these foreign variants including the LB-30A Liberator, LB-30B Liberator I and the later Liberator II for the RAF. The Liberator II was the first to incorporate the 3ft stretched nose called for by Reuben Fleet early in the Liberator's development. Sadly, the first production Liberator II crashed during a test flight, killing intrepid test pilot Wheatley.

Only nine B-24C Liberators were built and none actually saw service in the bombing role. Typical of the continuing refining of the type, these incorporated new 0.50in (12.7mm) twin machine-guns in a top turret behind the cockpit, as well as in a tail gun position. The relatively few 'C' model aircraft were used for training and development.

The B-24D version was for a long time the familiar configuration associated with the Liberator. This version was powered by 1,200hp Pratt & Whitney R-1830-43 engines except for late 'D' models produced in San Diego which used the -65. Like all Liberators, the B-24D had the distinctive flat oval engine cowlings which resulted from placing air scoops on each side of the engine. The Hamilton Standard three-bladed, fully feathering propellers were 11ft 7in (3.53m) in diameter.

To give a sample specification for the Liberator type, the B-24D had a wing span of 110ft (33.52m), length of 66ft 4in (20.22m), height of 17ft 11in (5.46m) and wing area of 1,048sq ft (97.36m²). The B-24D had a maximum speed of 303mph (488km/h), an initial climb rate of 1,100ft (335m) per min, and an impressive combat radius of 1,080 miles (1,730km).

The B-24D Liberator weighed 33,980lb (15,413kg) empty and maximum take-off weight was around 60,000lb (27,216kg). Maximum internal bomb load of the B-24D was 8,000lb (3,629kg).

On a historic note, a B-24D (41-23754) nicknamed 'Teggie Ann' and belonging to the 93rd Bomb Group, Eighth Air Force, was the first Liberator of any kind to fly over Nazi-occupied Europe, to the Fives-Lille steelworks in France on 9 October 1942. Sergeant Ernest Kish, this Liberator's tail-gunner, suffered frostbite struggling to free frozen guns, the sort of thing that was to happen repeatedly on high-altitude missions.

No solution was ever found for the terrible cold and almost unbearable discomfort inflicted on the crew, particularly those in the rear fuselage where the sides of the aircraft had to be opened-up for guns to protrude. It was not comfortable back there and stories of every manner of freezing and frostbite were legion.

One of the legends of the war in Europe concerns a B-24 Liberator which was disabled and surrounded by Nazi fighters and lowered its undercarriage in the recognized gesture of surrender. The story has it that the B-24 crew lured the Messerschmitts to within close range, sucked up the landing gear abruptly, and opened fire – thereby violating some code of chivalry which would have required the crew to let itself be escorted to a German base. According to the legend, German fighter forces then made a special target of the bomb group which had committed this heinous offence and inflicted very heavy casualties. The story is a good one and may have some foundation, but no record can be found of a Liberator faking its surrender in mid-air only to tempt Luftwaffe fighters to their destruction.

Together with B-17s, several B-24s were captured and flown by the Germans, both for the purpose of evaluating their adversary's equipment and for sneaking into American bomber formations.

Classic front view of the wartime Liberator – well, not precisely. This shot actually depicts a US Navy Liberator on 20 June 1952, perhaps the last twin-tailed ship to serve in the Navy. Originally designated PB4Y-1, the aircraft (bureau number 12382) had been converted for photo-reconnaissance duties and redesignated P4Y-1P while serving with Utility Squadron One (VU-1). (via Lt-Cdr Dave Parsons)

The Consolidated factory at Lindbergh Field in San Diego was always a small, cramped facility, and it became even more crowded as Liberators poured out of the doors. The B-24Ds seen ready for delivery include aircraft No 149 in the foreground, which is B-24D 42-40149. (USAF)

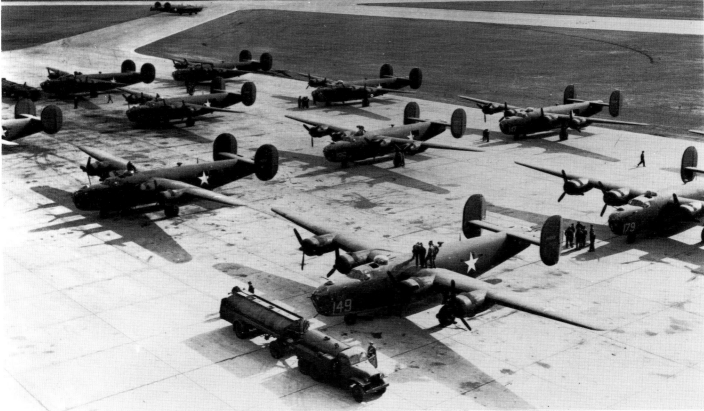

In the Pacific the 90th Bomb Group, the 'Jolly Rogers', of the US Fifth Air Force set up shop at Iron Ridge, Australia, in November 1942 and soon moved north to Guadalcanal where they began the long slog north towards Tokyo. In both theatres, the bomber generals struggling to put together a new kind of long-range aerial warfare were greatly relieved that production of the Liberator was proceeding.

When additional sources of production opened for the new bomber, Ford at Willow Run and Douglas at Tulsa turned out their carbon copies of the B-24D under the designation B-24E. North American's version was the B-24G.

The one-off XB-24F Liberator (41-11678), a converted 'D' model, was fitted in March 1943 with hot-air de-icing, a feature which might have proved useful had it been adopted operationally, since rubber boot de-icers could easily be rendered useless by shell fragments and thousands of man-hours were wasted inspecting them before missions. This machine was operated by the National Advisory Committee for Aeronautics (NACA) at Moffett Field, California.

In later years those who kept numerical tabs on the Allies' struggle against tyranny reported that the Liberator should have been designated a fighter since it shot down an impressive 2,600 Axis aircraft in air-to-air combat. It did not, of course, turn on them and chase them down – but its protective screen of flying steel could be lethal. Several instances have been verified of gunners becoming 'aces' by downing five enemy fighters.

## Armed Escort

One approach to the need for an escort fighter to protect bomber formations was the XB-41, a single aircraft based on a B-24D airframe (41-11822) which carried a massive defensive armament of fourteen 0.50in (12.7mm) machine-guns. Just as a YB-40 gunship had been developed from a Flying Fortress airframe, the XB-41 based on the Liberator was intended to serve as a bomber escort.

The concept of a 'convoy fighter' had been promoted by Elliott Roosevelt, who asked his friend Howard Hughes, Clarence (Kelly) Johnson at Lockheed, and key designers with other manufacturing firms to develop big, twin-engined fighters, but they never proved practical. If the job of 'convoying' heavy bomber formations could not be achieved by one of these aircraft – the Hughes D-2 or Lockheed XP-58 (both built in prototype form only) – perhaps the solution was to take the heavy armament envisaged for this mission and incorporate it in a bomber.

Tests of the XB-41 were carried out at Eglin Field, Florida, in the spring and summer of 1943, and initially the Army approved the manufacture of a small number of such aircraft. This was dropped, however, when it became apparent that such a 'flying gunship' with its heavy ammunition load was simply too heavy to maintain formation with the bombers it was supposed to escort. Furthermore, the 'convoy fighter' concept was overtaken by events as progress in stretching the range of escort fighters like the P-47 Thunderbolt and P-51 Mustang occurred much earlier than anticipated. Unlike the YB-40 Flying Fortress which reached England in small numbers, the XB-41 was never used operationally, but the question of how to arm and protect bombers persisted both before and during the war.

## Armament Issues

In fact, long after the United States entered the war there was still disagreement as to how bombers should be armed. Early Liberators had only ball-and-socket mounted, hand-held machine-guns which almost seemed a kind of afterthought, just one more duty for a busy crewman with other more demanding tasks. The idea of installing defensive gun turrets grew slowly in America, although they had long been common elsewhere. Not until late in the B-24D production run (with aircraft 41-1142) was an electrically operated, retractable Bendix lower turret installed in the Liberator. This was supplanted by a Briggs/Sperry ball turret with twin 0.50in (12.7mm) guns.

The power tail turret on the Liberator, manufactured by Motor Products, was also introduced with the B-24D model and remained standard later. With late B-24G models and continuing through the remainder of Liberator production, a nose turret became standard. The Motor Products nose turret, not before time, was replaced by the Emerson unit found in the nose of all late-model Liberators. None of these turrets was ever comfortable and some of them made the gunner's life hell in the cramped discomfort at high altitude; but turrets undoubtedly improved the effectiveness of the bomber's defences so the price had to be paid.

## H Model

Production of the Liberator by its parent company continued unabated after Reuben Fleet sold his interest in Consolidated in 1943. Merging with the Vultee firm to become Consolidated Vultee (and later abbreviated Convair), the maker of the B-24

Sitting alongside the fence, apparently at the San Diego factory, this camouflaged Consolidated B-24 Liberator exudes strength and power. It also has a pair of nose guns pointing straight ahead. The generals who ran the US air campaign kept searching for ways to increase the firepower of bomber formations, one approach being a heavily armed Liberator variant called the XB-41, but persistent Luftwaffe pilots were always able to get through, even when attacking from the front. (via Dave Ostrowski)

An early US Navy PB4Y-1 Liberator on patrol along the American coast. The nautical Liberator was ideal for long-range anti-submarine patrols and other missions which called for endurance. Subsequent PB4Y-2 and later models were named Privateer and had the single tail, which was also tested on several USAAF B-24 models. (via Lt-Cdr Dave Parsons)

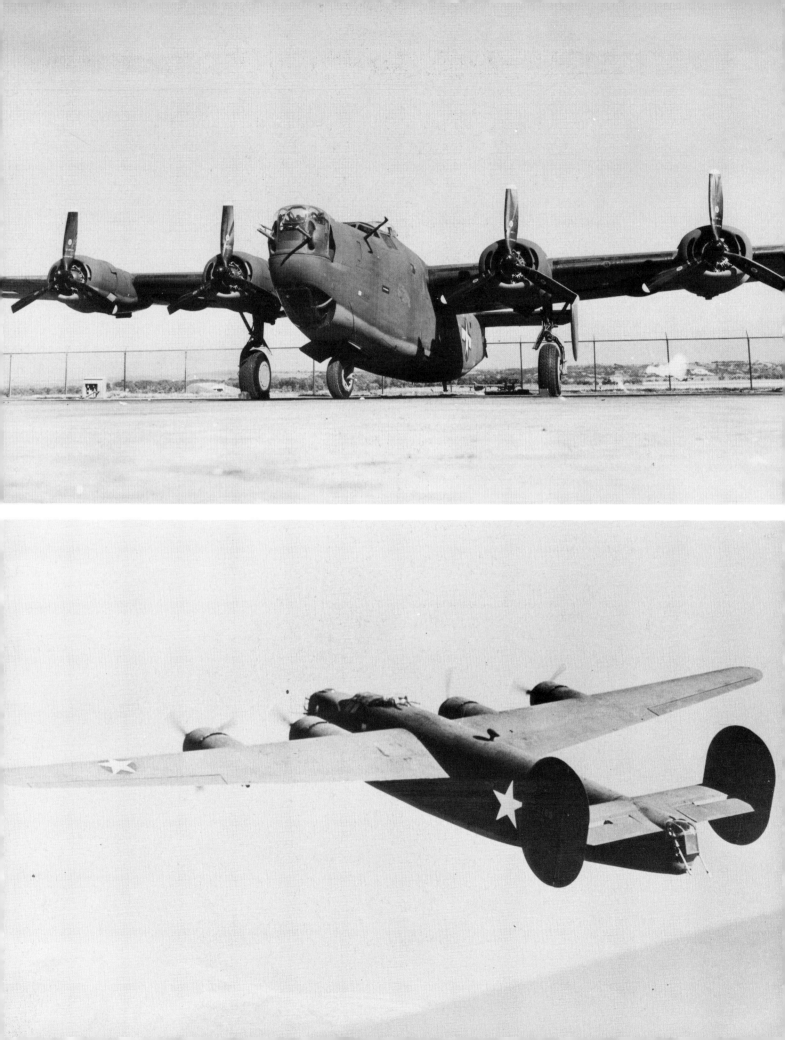

continued its predominant role. (In later years, the firm became the Convair Division of General Dynamics and, finally, the Convair identity was dropped altogether.)

The nose turret-equipped B-24H Liberator actually appeared before the turret-equipped B-24G, on 30 June 1943 with the delivery of the first Ford-manufactured 'H' model at Willow Run. From then on the Liberator's armament remained little changed, the bomber being able to place defensive fire around itself in almost a complete sphere.

By the time the 'H' model appeared, production of the Liberator was in full swing; the Willow Run facility alone was turning out a completed B-24H Liberator at the rate of one every 100 minutes, around the clock, seven days a week. 'Nowadays we tend to forget just how incredible that industrial machine really was,' says former Consolidated worker Dennis Gordon. 'We actually pushed them out the doors faster than folks could find places to park them. We would need to add some final item, like a strip of upholstery, and people would run up and down the tarmac putting this final touch on dozens of airplanes, one after another.'

Following on the heels of the B-24H came the B-24J, which also had the full gun turret armament and was heavier. Consolidated's second plant at Fort Worth, Texas, began producing the B-24J on 25 September 1943 and the 'J' model, the most numerous in the series, also rolled off the line at San Diego, Willow Run, Tulsa and Dallas. One result of this mass-production miracle was that Liberators from each builder were slightly different from all others, a situation highly exasperating for maintenance men; it was addressed but not solved by forming a tooling sub-committee of the B-24 Liaison Committee in September 1944.

Seemingly a radical departure at the time, the XB-24K, sometimes known as the B-24ST (for Single Tail), was an experimental conversion of a single B-24D (42-40058) Liberator fitted with a single vertical fin and first flown on 6 March 1943. This aircraft also introduced improved internal features and minor changes in armament. The B-24L was a production Liberator with minor changes from the 'J' model in armament and internal fittings. A variation was the Ford-built B-24M.

The B-24N was another single-tail version which reflected Consolidated efforts to continue developing the basic design. Improvements included longer engine nacelles housing larger oil tanks, an Emerson ball nose turret and lightweight ball turret in the tail, and a new cockpit window configuration enhancing the pilot's visibility. The first B-24N flew in November 1944 and seven of this version were actually com-

pleted. No fewer than 5,168 were ordered only to be cancelled as the war proceeded and other priorities beckoned.

The single XB-24P and XB-24Q were used for various systems tests. The latter was a Ford-built Liberator with a remotely sighted, radar-controlled tail gun stinger not unlike that eventually employed on post-war bombers such as the Boeing B-47 and B-52.

A number of Liberators were rebuilt to serve as cargo aircraft with the designation C-87 and C-87A. These soldiered valiantly, carrying cargoes across the Atlantic and Pacific, often under the most difficult circumstances, with far from satisfactory navigation aids and very unforgiving weight and balance

Fort Worth-built B-24J Liberator 44-10560 over Texas in its natural metal finish shortly after roll-out from the factory. This became the definitive configuration for the Liberator. A few of the aircraft in this series were leased to Britain and Canada. (via R. J. Mills, Jr)

tolerances. One C-87 mission was immortalized in Ernest K. Gann's novel *Fate Is The Hunter*. Other Liberators for the 'hauling' role were rebuilt as fuel tankers and designated C-109.

The latter may have enjoyed a reputation as the most dangerous aircraft of World War II. The designation C-109 went to fuel-tanker conversions of several variants of the B-24, beginning with an XC-109 test ship converted from a B-24E (42-72210) and denuded of all armour, armament and bombing equipment. The aircraft became a 'flying fuel tank' with containers installed in the nose, bomb bay (two) and rear fuselage (three), bringing fuel capacity up to 2,400 US gallons (which took a full hour to be pumped out of the aircraft). Used mostly in the CBI

(China-Burma-India) theatre to supply fuel to the China-based B-29 force, no fewer than 218 C-109s were converted and many were lost in fiery crashes.

To continue the roster of Liberator mods, the XF-7, F-7, F-7A and F-7B were photo-reconnaissance versions based, respectively, on the B-24D, B-24H, B-24J and (in the F-7B) late-model B-24J. The first XF-7 was a modification centre conversion of a B-24D Liberator (41-11653) achieved by removing all bombing equipment and installing eleven cameras in the nose, bomb bay and rear fuselage.

A few Liberators – one source gives the figure as five – were built as trainers under the designation AT-22. All of these had the configuration of the B-24D, built before nose turrets were added to the

A new B-24J Liberator flying through California mountains. The bar added to the US national insignia midway through the war helped to ease recognition problems. Waist gunners aboard this aircraft, their weapons poking out, have a spectacular ride. At high altitude it was also a very cold ride with frostbite an ever-present danger. (via Dave Ostrowski)

US Navy PB4Y-1 Liberator belonging to patrol squadron 106 (VB-106) cracked up at a South-West Pacific airfield in about 1944 and was deemed too badly damaged for repair. Members of the squadron are seen seeking to salvage what can be saved amid piles of scattered PSP (pierced steel planking). Naval aviators in the Liberator flew long and gruelling missions, often alone, and had to fend for themselves when trouble arose. (USN)

Built under licence by Douglas at Tulsa, Oklahoma, this B-24D Liberator (41-28411) wearing nose number '32' seems to have acquired a tremendous amount of wear and tear without ever receiving operational squadron markings; thousands of bombers were needed at stateside locations to support the thousands more which went abroad to fight. Lacking a nose turret, the B-24D version was soon replaced by later Liberators. (USAF)

familiar Liberator shape. They were used to train navigators who flew aboard the C-87 cargo aircraft. Later they were redesignated TB-24.

US Navy versions included the PB4Y-1 Liberator (with familiar twin tail) and the PB4Y-2 Privateer. The Privateer had a 7ft (2.1m) longer fuselage, single fin, vertical-ellipse engine cowlings, and revised armament, including an Erco nose turret and waist gun blisters. It is understood that range was increased and that crews regarded the type as ideal for long-endurance patrol missions over ocean expanses. The Navy's transport versions of the Liberator were the RY-1 and RY-2 (with twin tails), used rather extensively especially on the West Coast, followed by the RY-3 (with a single fin).

## Liberator Combat

In the European theatre the four-engined Consolidated bomber was often overshadowed by its better-known cousin from Boeing. In fact, when the Eighth Air Force set up shop in England, Fortresses greatly outnumbered Liberators at first. When round-the-clock bombing of the Reich got seriously under way in February 1943 (at about the time when it became clear that the US would persist with daylight bombing, while the RAF struck Germany at night), the balance was changing. In time the Liberator

became a full partner in the long aerial struggle against Hitler.

Following 'Teggie Ann's' first mission, on 21 November 1942 a Liberator flown by Major Ramsey Potts came under attack by five Junkers Ju 88s. Far from succumbing to their guns, the Liberator shot down two Ju 88s, damaged another, and escaped. Liberators mounted small-scale missions against targets in the Ruhr and, when confronted by fighters, invariably managed to defend themselves.

During the sustained assaults against Reich targets in July 1943, known as 'Blitz Week', Liberators were again overshadowed by Fortresses, but Luftwaffe casualties scarcely noticed. During the 'Big Week' of 19–25 February 1944, which saw even greater masses of bombers heading deep into Germany, Liberators again carried their part of the load.

It all culminated with the Eighth Air Force launching its biggest mission of the war, the 24 December 1944 Christmas Eve strikes against Rhineland targets. Every serviceable B-17 and B-24 was sent, a total of 2,034 bombers. Lt. Stephen Wamburg of the 458th Bomb Group piloted a Liberator. 'It was a relatively calm mission for my crew except for some problems with ice forming inside the aircraft. We never came close to getting hit by flak or fighters. But at one time shortly after take-off, crossing the English coast, we had [a] most spectacular view of a major part of the attack force – hundreds of Fortresses and Liberators streaming into Europe.'

Formations employing the Liberator in Europe included the 34th, 44th, 93rd, 389th, 392nd, 445th, 446th, 448th, 453rd, 458th, 466th, 467th, 486th, 487th, 489th, 490th, 491st, 492nd and 493rd Bomb Groups. The 491st Bomb Group, 'Ringmasters', achieved the highest rate of sorties over Germany of all B-24 groups.

In Mediterranean operations, the B-24 Liberator is best known for its long-range raids against the oilfields at Ploesti, Rumania, which then produced some 2.5 per cent of the world's refined fuel oil. The Halverson Detachment, also known as 'Halpro', was the first Liberator unit to fly in the Mediterranean. Originally formed to strike Japan from Chinese bases, 'Halpro' operated from the RAF airfield at Fayid near the Suez Canal in Egypt and mounted a strike on Ploesti on 12 June 1942. It was the first American bombing raid on a target in Europe. Only thirteen bombers went on the mission and only seven returned – far from a successful beginning.

The 98th and 376th Bomb Groups soon reinforced the 'Halpro' aircraft and were in turn bolstered by the 44th and 93rd Groups. In April 1943 General Henry H. (Hap) Arnold ordered the first efforts at what became known as Operation 'Tidal Wave', a mass low-level strike on Ploesti using all these formations of B-24D Liberators.

## Ploesti Raid

On 1 August 1943 the 'Tidal Wave' mission was launched, the first B-24D being flown by Brig.-Gen. Uzal G. Ent. To avoid detection the mission was flown at very low level, altitude over the target varying from 50 to 300ft (15 to 91m). It was gruelling. The 1,500-mile (2,500km) round-trip from bases in North Africa ran into stiff German resistance and forty-one B-24Ds were lost in action. Twelve more of the 164 aircraft in the strike force were lost to other causes.

Colonel William R. Cameron remembers Liberators from several bomb groups converging from different directions over Ploesti in a terrifying affirmation of Murphy's Law ('If something can go wrong, it will'). As he flew towards the refinery known as Columbia Aguila, Cameron peered with apprehension at a companion B-24. The other aircraft's target was exactly in line with the spot where Cameron's own bombs were programmed to fall. With his gunners popping off machine-gun bursts at a train beneath him, and other Liberators threatening to collide, Cameron realized that he could not manoeuvre his aircraft without causing a mid-air collision and bringing destruction to his own crew and others. So he held his B-24 level, dropped his bombs, and fought his way out through a half-dozen Messerschmitts.

'Ruthless Ruthie', a Consolidated B-24J Liberator (44-40317) stationed at North Pickenham, Norfolk, England, suffered misfortune on 17 April 1945 and ended up belly upon ground, port wing looming skyward. It is not clear whether 'Ruthie' had this experience following a combat mission. From what is visible, the Liberator could probably have been repaired and returned to service. (USAF)

The Liberator crews had flown against some of the most concentrated defences in the world and no fewer than five men were awarded Medals of Honor for the mission, including Colonel Leon Johnson of the 44th Bomb Group and John ('Killer') Kane, skipper of the 98th Bomb Group. Two weeks later the same Liberator groups had more success attacking the Messerschmitt assembly plant at Wiener-Neustadt in Austria, but it was Ploesti that beckoned. Several further strikes by Liberators whittled away at the Germans' oil capacity.

The Ninth, Twelfth and Fifteenth Air Forces never achieved the same acclaim as the British-based Eighth Air Force, but the Liberators which fought on the southern flank of Europe had a difficult war. As pilots of the 376th Bomb Group discovered at rain-drenched San Pancrazio airfield in Italy, the weather in the region was of only two varieties – bad and bad. For an extended period, the airfield was a virtual lake and the Liberator could be operated only because it could 'swim'.

The Fifteenth Air Force had been formed in 1943 under Brig. Gen. James H. Doolittle, leader of the famous Tokyo raid, and comprised half-a-dozen groups divided equally between Fortresses and Liberators. By early 1944 the Fifteenth was established at a complex of airstrips around Foggia and Bari and was carrying out short-range missions on the Italian battle front. It was also flying deeper

strikes against rail yards, airfields and industrial targets in Austria, Bulgaria, Rumania and Yugoslavia. These were far from 'milk runs', no matter how Fortress crews in England might have characterized them, and a disproportionate number of these Liberator crewmen were shot down and taken prisoner.

Typical was a series of missions beginning on 2 April 1944 when Fortresses and Liberators attacked the Steyr-Daimler-Puch ball-bearing plant and its associated Luftwaffe airfields. Gunners aboard the Liberators claimed to have shot down more than 100 Messerschmitt Me 109Gs. 204 tons of incendiaries and 550 tons of high-explosive were dropped, but twenty bombers were shot down and thirty limped home damaged. As April wore on, several raids were mounted against the Ploesti oilfields, one of them enabling 290 B-17s and B-24s to drop 793 tons of bombs. As 1944 wore on, the Axis in Italy shrank and, in due course, Liberators were doing 'mop up' operations in the area.

Mediterranean theatre Liberator combat formations included the 98th, 376th, 449th, 450th, 451st, 454th, 455th, 456th, 459th, 460th, 461st, 464th, 465th, 484th and 485th Bomb Groups. Best known may have been the 450th, the 'Cotton Tails', which began operations at Manduria, Italy, in December 1943 and flew especially difficult missions over Regensburg and Ploesti. The US Navy also operated

Camouflaged Consolidated B-24H Liberator 42-52317 'Leila Bell', with hash marks to indicate completed missions but without individual unit insignia, in a formation which includes aircraft (background) in natural metal finish. The B-24H model had a powered nose turret but did not have many of the internal and structural improvements found on the B-24J. (USAF)

Consolidated B-24D Liberator 42-72843 'Strawberry Bitch' belonging to the US Air Force Museum was overhauled at Davis-Monthan AFB, Arizona, when seen there in natural metal on 26 March 1959, had been fully repainted when seen at the same location running up engines for its last flight on 29 April 1959 and was flown to Dayton, Ohio where it made a trip on the ground when the museum changed locations in January 1971. 'Strawberry Bitch' remains a splendid memorial to all the B-24s of the conflict. (USAF)

US Air Force flight crew member John Vadas stands in front of yet another preserved Liberator, B-24J 'Delectable Doris', on 8 August 1976 at MacDill Air Force Base, Florida. (John Vadas)

several squadrons of PB4Y-1 Liberators in the Mediterranean area during the war.

In the Pacific, where the Liberator island-hopped along with Allied troops as they drew closer to Japan, the Consolidated bomber snubbed its nose at fighters and gave its crews an excellent prospect for getting out alive when they got into a tight situation.

General George C. Kenney noted that the B-24 carried more bombs than the B-17, had greater range, and could, if necessary, be flown when seriously overloaded. Outfits like the 307th Bomb Group, the 'Long Rangers', moved from Hickam to Wake Island to Guadalcanal to New Georgia, and ultimately to Clark Field in the Philippines. On long over-water missions, combat pilots and crews were delighted that the Liberator offered excellent endurance and survivability.

B-24 combat units in the Pacific included the 5th, 7th, 11th, 22nd, 28th, 30th, 43rd, 90th, 307th, 308th, 380th and 494th Bomb Groups. The last-named, 'Kelly's Kobras', was the final Liberator group to be activated and fought through to Okinawa where its last strikes were directed against occupied China and Korea. A number of US Navy and Marine Corps squadrons operated PB4Y-1 Liberators and PB4Y-2 Privateers on combat missions.

Remarkably, despite the numbers in which it was built, the B-24 Liberator was another of those types for which no post-war role was envisaged by the soon-to-be independent US Air Force. Vast numbers of Liberators were junked or left to rot in places like the aircraft boneyard in Kingman, Arizona. A few foreign air arms managed to operate Liberators, including those of China and India, while the French Navy acquired some Privateers.

Naval variants of the Liberator remained in service for a time longer. In the 1950s Privateers were known as P4Ys, versions including the P4Y-2K target. This Navy version even survived through the 1961 change in the US military designation system to become the P-4. A few Privateers went to the US Coast Guard as the PB4Y-2G. One Privateer on an intelligence-gathering mission was shot down by Soviet fighters in 1948 and a few served in the 1950–53 Korean War.

An early B-24D Liberator, nicknamed 'Strawberry Bitch', found its way to the US Air Force Museum in Dayton, Ohio. A Ford-built Liberator (44-51228) employed in de-icing experiments at Robins AFB, Georgia, acquired the unlikely designation EZB-24M and eventually ended up on display at Lackland AFB, Texas, where it remains today. Thanks to the almost single-handed efforts of Eighth Air Force Museum Curator Harold D. (Buck) Rigg, a long-hidden but nearly immaculate B-24J (44-48781) will soon be on display at the museum at Barksdale AFB, Louisiana.

# SBD Dauntless

There are those who insist that the Battle of Midway was the most important event in the war against Japan. True or not, rarely has such a historical turning point owed so much to a single type of aircraft.

A handful of Dauntlesses made the difference. It happened near the end of the day, far from the aircraft-carriers from which they had come and which offered safe haven, amidst a crisis of malfunctioning electrical systems, with fuel and daylight running out, with what seemed almost no chance of success, this handful of Dauntlesses suddenly came upon the Japanese fleet. With all the odds against them, the Dauntlesses swarmed down on Admiral Yamamoto's carriers, *Hiryu, Soryu, Kaga, Akagi* . . .

Seldom in history has a turning point been so clear, so decisive.

One of the grand old men of aviation, designer Jack Northrop, who later pioneered flying-wing bombers, ought to receive the lion's share of credit for the Dauntless. The SBD Dauntless traces its ancestry in large measure to Northrop's two-seat, low-wing BT-1 dive-bomber of 1938 and to the experimental XBT-2 variant which followed. Founded in 1932, the Northrop Aircraft Company of El Segundo, California, was controlled financially by Douglas and became a part of the Douglas conglomerate when Jack Northrop left the firm in January 1938.

The Dauntless came into being because Jack Northrop's achievements fitted nicely into what amounted to a serial partnership between Northrop and Douglas Aircraft's widely acclaimed Edward H. Heinemann.

Few designers are better known than Heinemann, who has at times seemed to court recognition, but he would be the first to acknowledge that developing an aircraft is a team effort. Heinemann instructed his people to rework the sole XBT-2 (bureau number 0627). They had the benefit of considerable experience because Douglas engineers had been looking at the scout/dive-bomber idea since 1934, when the US Navy circulated new specifications for a dive-bomber which – remarkably, for the era – did not have to be a biplane.

The BT-1 had been one of no fewer than six designs submitted to the Navy not merely by Northrop but also by Brewster, Curtiss, Great Lakes, Martin and Vought.

On paper, a similar but larger aeroplane took shape, powered by a 1,000hp Wright XR-1830-32 engine, precursor of the world-famous Cyclone, driving a three-bladed propeller. A new shape was adopted for the vertical tail and the XBT-2 became the XSBD Dauntless. At that time design work was also well advanced on the Curtiss SB2C Helldiver (a contemporary of and not, as was later understood, a replacement for, the Dauntless). 'The Beast', as Curtiss's product was to become known to pilots, was no competition. The SBD Dauntless was to become the ideal carrier-based scout bomber, setting a standard against which all others would be judged.

It was this aircraft which determined the configuration for all Navy scout bombers for years to come. Control surface area ratios, fin configurations, wing shape and numerous other features of the Buccaneer, Vengeance, Helldiver and others were determined by the configuration of this aeroplane.

## Scout Bomber

Sometimes forgotten is the fact that the Dauntless was designed specifically for a dual mission, the

The XBT-2, which began life as the XBT-1, was designed by Jack Northrop and served as the progenitor not only of the immortal SBD Dauntless but of all wartime US dive-bombers. Dug up by Lt-Cdr Dave Parsons of the US Navy's Flight Safety Center, this rare view depicts the sole XBT-2, bureau number 0627, in flight on 1 September 1938. (USN via Parsons)

The classic lines of a thoroughbred. US Marine Corps Douglas SBD-4 Dauntless (bureau number 18780) at an airfield on the East Coast between June 1942 and June 1943. In typical Marine glossy sea blue with lighter tones as well, this particular Dauntless has an eager-looking crew (almost certainly posed), but its only payload is a Mark 43 practice bomb under the starboard wing. (via Lt-Cdr Dave Parsons)

'scout' portion calling for a second crew member to perform visual reconnaissance while the 'bomber' portion could, conceivably, have been accomplished by a single-seat aircraft. The role of carrier-based aircraft has changed at several key junctures over the years. At the beginning of the war, a scout bomber was intended to prowl at extended range away from the carrier force, find the enemy, and attack him.

The Dauntless was also, of course, a dive-bomber, designed to launch its attack by boring straight down out of the sky and dropping its deadly payload on the enemy with greater accuracy than could normally be achieved by high level bombing.

The Dauntless's centre-line bomb was held by a hinged yoke which, on release, swung the bomb forward and down so as to clear the arc of the propeller. Under the pre-war tactics developed by the US Navy, the truly aggressive dive-bomber pilot was supposed to make his run on the target flying straight down at maximum speed. As the Dauntless evolved, improvements were made in the bomb sight which permitted the pilot to do this.

The second crewman became a gunner with one, later two, flexible 0.50in (12.7mm) machine-guns. Because he faced to the rear of the aircraft, his back to the pilot, boring straight down at a Japanese ship was an especially unsettling experience for him! Gunners in the Dauntless became adept at shooting

down Japanese aircraft and their role was lauded in story and song, the most famous Dauntless gunner being the character Roscoe Sweeney in the popular American 'Buz Sawyer' comic strip. What was often forgotten, however, was that the second crewman was there primarily because of the scout mission, his skill with machine-guns being secondary.

In truth, almost every aspect of American carrier aviation was in the developmental stage as war approached. The Dauntless was by no means the only carrier-based dive-bomber under development, nor even the only monoplane. Britain had developed the Blackburn Skua, the Fleet Air Arm's first monoplane, and in April 1940 aircraft of this type dive-bombed and sank the German cruiser *Königsberg*, the first major warship to succumb to this form of attack.

## Brewster Entry

The Brewster company had its own experience with dive-bombers and hoped to win a sizable order from the Navy.

The pre-war Brewster SBA-1 had been the US Navy's first monoplane dive-bomber. First flown on 15 April 1936 and powered by a 950hp Wright XR-1820-22 Cyclone radial, after unsuccessful trials with the 750hp Wright R-1820-3, the SBA-1 was pro-

Dauntlesses in flight over the Pacific on 26 June 1942. Gunner of second aircraft has his canopy closed, but crew members usually preferred the open air, even though engine fumes could become a hazard. These Dauntlesses are not carrying bombs and could be returning from a combat mission. (USN)

The Brewster Aeronautical Company produced some uninspiring designs and by March 1944, when this Brewster SB2A-1 Buccaneer was flying over the Pacific, the firm was already going out of business. The Buccaneer was intended as a dive-bomber but never entered combat. (USN)

duced in small numbers not by its designer but by the Naval Aircraft Factory under the designation SBN-1. Not a successful aircraft, it was in a training role long before the war began.

The Brewster SB2A-1 Buccaneer was better known, but not by much. Not dissimilar in external appearance to the Dauntless but larger and with a wider landing-gear track, the Buccaneer was ordered in prototype form by the Navy on 4 April 1939 and flew on 17 June 1941.

The Buccaneer was powered by a 1,700hp Wright R-2600-8 Cyclone radial and seems, in part, to have been procured as a backstop to the Dauntless, lest the latter fail in operational service. The US Navy eventually ordered eighty SB2A-2s, and sixty SB2A-3s having minor differences, as well as applying the designation SB2A-4 to 162 aircraft ordered by the Dutch Army Air Force in the Netherlands East Indies, which fell to the Japanese before the machines could be delivered. The aircraft was given the Air Corps designation A-34, although the latter service never obtained any, and the bulk (around 750) went to the RAF as the Bermuda. Although 771 of these aeroplanes were manufactured, so far as can be determined none actually participated in combat; the RAF used them as target tugs. So formidable was the Dauntless that anything else was strictly second-rate.

To return to the Dauntless story, in February 1939 the US Navy formally accepted the XSBD-1. Two months later on 8 April 1939, the Navy ordered 57 SBD-1 aircraft for the Marine Corps and 87 SBD-2s for Navy squadrons.

## Pilot View

From the viewpoint of the pilot who would take it into battle, the Dauntless was a revolution. The Dauntless pilot found himself seated high up front in a classic 'taildragger' aeroplane of all-metal construction with fabric-covered control surfaces. His cantilever, low-mounted wing had a rectangular centre-section with outer panels tapering in chord and thickness to detachable wing tips. The 'Swiss cheese' pierced flaps and dive-brakes, above and below the trailing edge of the outer wings and below the trailing edge only of the centre-section beneath the fuselage, together with the multi-cellular construction of the wing itself, were telltale indicators of the design's indebtedness to Jack Northrop.

The Dauntless's oval duralumin monocoque fuselage was built in four sections; the crew was housed beneath a continuous transparent canopy with a bullet-proof windshield and armour plate. The swinging bomb cradle could accommodate a single bomb of up to 1,000lb (454kg) and was centred

Carrying a bomb under the centre-line on a December 1943 mission, a Dauntless flies over burning fires on Wake Island, the Pacific atoll where American forces were sorely defeated by Japanese invaders earlier in the war. Wake's importance is illustrated by the fact that as late as the early 1960s, it was an essential staging point for propeller-driven airliners crossing the Pacific. Even today the relic of a sunken Japanese ship remains in the lagoon. (USN)

An SBD Dauntless, apparently without sufficient fuel to return to its carrier, ditches in the Pacific beside a US Navy cruiser on 4 June 1942. The impact appears brutal, but the pilot and gunner were rescued by boat. (USN)

A lifetime later this Dauntless is on display at the World War II exhibit of the US Marine Corps Museum at Quantico, Virginia. The aircraft is actually a former USAAF A-24B Dauntless (42-54582) which has been restored and painted to represent a Marine aircraft. The aircraft is shown complete with machine-guns and bombs, although the USAAF's Dauntlesses did very little machine-gunning or bombing of anyone. (USMC)

beneath the fuselage with a bomb rack mounted also under each outer-wing section.

A reasonably able pilot flying the Dauntless found it to be a forgiving aeroplane with relatively few vices, although it had a troublesome tendency to stall in tight turns. On dive-bombing missions, the pilot approached his target at 15,000 to 20,000ft (4,570 to 6,095m), took position almost directly overhead, pulled up the nose, and deployed upper and lower dive flaps. He then rolled in, the Dauntless accelerating less rapidly than might be expected while plummeting downwards at any angle from 70deg to full vertical. From the SBD-5 model on, the Dauntless was equipped with the Mark VIII reflector sight, replacing the earlier extended telescope which had a tendency to fog over in a dive as a result of temperature changes. Using this, the pilot aimed his bomb load by the simple expedient of aiming his aircraft at the target. His bomb release was a red button marked 'B' on the top of the stick and he could drop his ordnance singly or in salvo. The Dauntless also carried two 0.50in (12.7mm) fixed machine-guns in the nose but it was far from practical to fire these while at the same time trying to aim and dive-bomb.

If the pilot did not succumb to 'target fascination', which could lull him into failing to pull out in time, his Dauntless would handle quite well with its bomb

load gone and would pull out with a gentle pull on the stick. The Dauntless handled well in normal flight and the pilot's visibility was excellent, both when level and when descending for a tricky carrier landing. The Dauntless was also an exceptionally sturdy aircraft and many of them got the crew safely home after suffering heavy battle damage.

## SBD-1 Model

The first Dauntless variant, the SBD-1 – with the definitive fin and rudder shape for the Dauntless type –was the first to be armed with two forward-firing guns in the engine cowling, although these were 0.30in (7.62mm). The SBD-1 had only a single 0.30in (7.62mm) gun for the second crewman. Not yet fully cleared for shipboard operations, the SBD-1 went to land-based Marine squadrons and was delivered from June 1940 onwards.

The Navy SBD-2 differed from the Marine SBD-1 in having a second 0.30in (7.62mm) machine-gun for the second crewman (ever after to be called a 'gunner', despite his scout role) and armour protection around the cockpit. The SBD-2 model also had self-sealing rubber-lined metal fuel tanks and two additional 65 US-gal fuel tanks in the outer wing panels. The first machine in this batch (bureau number 2102) was handed over to the Navy in

## SBD DAUNTLESS

November 1940 and deliveries were completed by May 1941.

There remained key figures in high places who had yet to be convinced of the value of the dive-bomber, some of these being the same people who wondered if the United States ought to be preparing for any war at all. The Navy was investing modestly in torpedo-bombers such as the Douglas TBD-1 Devastator. There was some interest in shore-based, long-range patrol aircraft, not least because the Air Corps had shown up the Navy by demonstrating the B-17 Flying Fortress as a potential guardian of the nation's coasts. But neither then nor later was the dive-bomber ever a terribly important part of American thinking, and in 1941 the Truman Committee recommended that dive-bombers not be developed in quantity.

The German defeat of the French forces, highlighted by film of stormtroopers entering Paris and punctuated by the scream of descending Stukas, may not have convinced anyone whose mind was already made up, but it could not have failed to sway the undecided. Would a force of dive-bombers have prevented the fall of France? Almost certainly not, but it is interesting that a few Curtiss SBC-4 biplane dive-bombers were en route to that beleaguered country when the end came. Because of the US neutrality embargo, the camouflaged SBC-4s (technically CW-77Fs, being the export version) had to be shipped via Canada where they were loaded aboard the French carrier *Béarn* for onward shipment. France was overrun before these dated warplanes could reach the scene and the carrier was diverted to the West Indies where the Curtiss biplanes rotted in the tropical sun.

The US Navy forged ahead, ordering 174 Dauntlesses as the SBD-3. The SBD-3 variant had improved armour and electrical system and bladder-type self-sealing fuel tanks. By now the familiar Dauntless shape was established. The scout bomber had a maximum speed of 252mph (406km/h) in level flight, increasing to 276mph (444km/h) in a dive, a range of 1,225 miles (1,971km) with – or 1,370 miles (2,205km) without – a bomb load and a service ceiling of 27,100ft (8,260m).

Wing span of the Dauntless was 41ft 6½in (12.66m), length 33ft 1¼in (10.09m), height 13ft 7in (4.14m) and wing area 325sq ft (30.19m$^2$). A typical aircraft weighed 6,533lb (2,963kg) empty and had a maximum take-off weight of 10,700lb (4,854kg). None of the dimensions or performance figures was breathtaking, but the Dauntless was to be a steady success throughout the war. In addition to Brewster's entries, a few other divebombers came on the scene briefly but were not able to endure.

**Left:** The traditional view of an SBD Dauntless going into its dive-bomb mode. Accomplished dive-bomber pilots bragged of being able to bore straight down into the smoke stacks of Japanese warships. At Midway, the sinking of four Japanese aircraft-carriers by Dauntlesses inflicted a crippling blow and reversed the tide of the war. (USN)

**Right:** An SBD Dauntless (foreground) and five TBD Devastator torpedo-bombers line up to take off from the carrier USS *Enterprise* (CV-6) in the South Pacific on 4 May 1942. At lower left (centre), ahead of the Dauntless's wing leading edge, a launch officer is making arm signals and supervising one take-off every 30 seconds. Many of the aircrew who launched from *Enterprise* for combat failed to return. (USN)

**Below left:** Douglas SBD-5 Dauntless dive-bombers returning from a bombing run on the airfield at Param Island, Truk Atoll, on 29 April 1944. It was a highly personalized war for the Dauntless pilot. His shipmates aboard the aircraft-carrier in many instances never saw the enemy at all – indeed, entire fleets exchanged gunfire and air strikes from beyond visual range – but in a Dauntless it was impossible to avoid seeing every detail of the action that went on below. (USN)

**Right:** Perhaps unaware that war lies only five weeks ahead, SBD Dauntless crews of Scouting Squadron Six (VC-6) fly in formation over the USS *Enterprise* (CV-6). Unfortunately for the Japanese, *Enterprise* was not in port at Pearl Harbor five weeks later. The Dauntless dive-bomber was equipped with perforated dive brakes which were sometimes called 'cheese graters'. (USN)

## Vought Vindicator

Vought had manufactured the SBU-1 biplane bomber for the Navy in the 1930s and in 1935 received an order for two prototype XSB2U-1 monoplanes for US Navy evaluation, these being delivered in 1936.

On 26 October 1936 the US Navy ordered 54 production SB2U-1 machines. The SB2U-1 had an all-metal structure with part-fabric and part-metal skin and was powered by an 825hp Pratt & Whitney R-1535-96 Twin Wasp Junior engine.

The nickname 'Vindicator' was first given to the SB2U-2 version and to all which followed. The SB2U-2, of which 58 were built, and the SB2U-3 (57 built) introduced various improvements in armour, fuel load and electrical systems. A single aircraft tested on floats was designated SB2U-3. A number of similar Vought V-156 aircraft were delivered to the French before the fall of France and 50 V-156B-1s were supplied to Britain for use by the Fleet Air Arm, which named the type 'Chesapeake'.

Unlike the Dauntless, the Vindicator did not have a major effect on the war. A few SB2U aeroplanes were on the scene during the Battle of Midway but contributed little. Although it had a respectable maximum speed of 243mph (391km/h) at 9,500ft (2,895m), the Vindicator's part-fabric surfaces and its overall sluggishness rendered the aircraft a prime target for Japanese fighters. Like the British Chesapeakes, which served in a training capacity with Nos 728 and 811 Squadrons, the US Navy's Vindicators were quickly removed from carrier decks, relegated to non-combat duties, and eventually abandoned.

The sudden Japanese attack at Pearl Harbor on 7 December 1941 destroyed a number of SBD Dauntlesses on the ground, most of them belonging to the Marine Corps, although at least one got aloft to join the handful of American aeroplanes which challenged the onslaught.

This was the first and last time that the Dauntless suffered such an indignity. More typical of the Dauntless was a voice message which went to the US Fleet on 7 May 1942 during the Battle of the Coral Sea when a lone Dauntless pilot radioed, 'Scratch one flat-top. This is Dixon to Carrier, scratch one flat-top.'

Lt. Cdr. Robert Dixon, skipper of Bombing Squadron Two (VB-2), was reporting the sinking of the Japanese aircraft-carrier *Shoho* by warplanes from the American carriers *Lexington* and *Yorktown*. Dixon's announcement was the prelude to the turn of the tide which came on 4 June 1942 at Midway.

In that heroic engagement, the odds seemed stacked against the Dauntless crews. Launched from Admiral Chester Nimitz's carrier groups to seek out

The Vought SB2U Vindicator did little to vindicate the investment of the Vought-Sikorsky firm into this very conventional scout bomber design. Like the Buccaneer, the Vindicator did not accomplish much in combat and was relegated to second-line service. (via Lt-Cdr Dave Parsons)

those of Admiral Isoroku Yamamoto, they were running out of fuel, running out of daylight, and stretched to the limits of range when they came upon the enemy fleet and attacked. Lt. Cdr. C. Wade McClusky, Cdr Max Leslie and the other fliers from Scout Squadron Five (VS-5) and Bombing Three (VB-3) on the USS *Yorktown* and VS-8 and VB-8 on the USS *Hornet* lost 40 of their 128 dive-bombers swarming down on the Japanese carrier force, but by sending four enemy carriers to the bottom of the sea they reversed the course of the conflict. But even this epic achievement was in one sense a prelude: by VJ-Day, the Dauntless had sunk a greater tonnage of Japanese shipping than had any other aircraft in the Pacific War.

## Shipboard Bomber

Apart from two squadrons of SBDs, one each in the scouting and bombing roles, a typical US Navy carrier air group of the era consisted of two squadrons of fighters (Grumman F4F Wildcats or F6F Hellcats), one of torpedo-bombers (Douglas TBD Devastators, later Grumman TBF Avengers) and the two Dauntless units. The scouting mission had been conceived before the invention of radar, with which American carriers were equipped from the beginning of the war against Japan, while the Japanese were not. In practice, there was little

difference between the missions flown by the scout (VS) and bombing (VB) squadrons.

To continue the roster of variants, the SBD-4 version of the Dauntless, delivered to the Navy between October 1942 and April 1943 (some 780 being built), came to the Fleet with an electric fuel pump, improved radio navigation aids, and a Hamilton Standard Hydromatic constant-speed, fully feathering propeller.

Soon afterwards came the SBD-5 powered by an improved R-1820-60 engine providing 1,200hp. The two nose cowling guns of the SBD-5 model were of 0.50in (12.7mm) size. The latter was the definitive version of the Douglas dive-bomber, with no fewer than 2,965 pouring off the production lines between February 1943 and April 1944. One of these acquired the designation XSBD-6 with the installation of a 1,350hp Wright R1820-66 Cyclone, the most advanced version of the Dauntless powerplant. 450 production SBD-6 aircraft came off the line.

As each new version emerged from the factory, it became clear that the Dauntless was unique. It was one of the few aeroplanes which came off the line trouble-free, went to the Fleet trouble-free, and stayed that way. Other manufacturers were to admire the way this Douglas product moved into the hands of its operators so easily and adapted to the trials of combat so smoothly. Other aircraft types took longer.

## Curtiss's Product

The Curtiss SB2C Helldiver, which took so long to enter service that it actually replaced the Dauntless in some squadrons, was actually a contemporary of the Douglas aircraft and was not a particularly innovative or original machine. The name 'Helldiver' had been applied to earlier Curtiss biplane types of the 1930s, but the real Helldiver came into existence to meet a 1938 Navy specification under which it was in competition with the even more lacklustre Brewster Buccaneer.

The Helldiver, in fact, was ordered into production on 29 November 1940 before anyone even saw what the aircraft looked like. The first Curtiss Model 84 or XSB2C-1 Helldiver (bureau number 1758) made its maiden flight on 18 December 1940, a rather impressive aircraft in natural finish. Powered by a 1,700hp Wright R-2600-8 Cyclone 14, the aircraft performed well but was lost in a mishap in early

January 1941. In June 1942 the first production SB2C-1 took to the air and the programme continued.

In April 1941 the US Army ordered 900 Helldivers as the A-25 Shrike. Only a few actually entered service, the remainder being diverted to the hapless US Marines, who always seemed the recipient of everybody's last choice, as the SB2C-1A. Meanwhile, although production SB2C-1s began to reach Navy scouting squadrons as early as December 1942, it was at least another year before any signficant number were in service. The Dauntless had to fight at Coral Sea, Midway and Guadalcanal without any help from the Helldiver.

Versions of the Curtiss 'Beast' included the XSB2C-2, an experimental twin-float seaplane variant (one built); the SB2C-3 production machine (1,112 built); the SB2C-4 which proved to be the major production variant (1,985 built); the SB2C-5

On 15 August 1945, the historic day when it all came to an end, a four-plane division of SB2C Helldivers from the USS *Ticonderoga* (CV-14) returns from the carrier's final air strike on the Japanese home islands. Jettisonable fuel tanks were a 'must' for such missions. (USN)

Three decades after its service in World War II, what may be the last flyable Helldiver appears at an air show at Olathe, Kansas, on 7 June 1974. This Curtiss SB2C-5 (bureau number 83589, civil registration N92879) belong to the Confederate Air Force's Ghost Squadron at Harlingen, Texas. Internal bomb bay doors are partially open. (Clyde Gerdes)

Opened-up SB2C Helldiver in low-level flight over the Pacific. This was the final 'scout bomber' to have a second man functioning as a radioman and gunner (and in this instance, as a photographer) in the back seat. Post-war aircraft performing this mission were single-seaters. (USN)

A US Navy SB2C Helldiver in flight during World War II. (USN)

US Navy SB2C Helldivers in
flight during World War II.
(USN)

(970 built); and the XSB2C-6, an enlarged experimental version (two built). The aircraft was manufactured by Canadian Car & Foundry Company under licence with the designations SBW-1 (40 built); SBW-1B, this being the British Helldiver I (26 built, but never employed operationally in British service); SBW-3 (413 built); SBW-4 (96 built) and SBW-5 (86 built). Fairchild also manufactured a few Helldivers under the designations SBF-1 (50 built), SBF-3 (150 built), and SBF-4 (100 built).

A typical variant, the SB2C-4, had a wing span of 49ft 9in (15.16m), evidence that it was a far larger aircraft than many realized. Fuselage length was 36ft 8in (11.18m), height 13ft 2in (4.01m) and wing area 442sq ft (39.20m$^2$). The Helldiver had an empty weight of 10,547lb (4,784kg) and a maximum take-off weight of 16,616lb (7,537kg). The aircraft was credited with a maximum speed of 295mph (475km/h), service ceiling of 31,000ft (9,448m), and range of 1,165 miles (1,875km).

The Helldiver retained the now-familiar dive-bomber configuration except that the rear gunner's position was flush with the contour of the fuselage. Although it was criticized and lambasted, the nickname 'Beast' often being uttered without humour, the Helldiver actually proved of great value to the Navy in the Pacific near the end of the war. With more than 7,000 Helldivers built in all, many of them later exported to foreign Allies in the post-war years, it is perhaps unfortunate that the type was so overshadowed by the Dauntless.

## Army Dive-Bombers

In the US Army Air Forces the Dauntless was officially known as the A-24 Banshee, although its more familiar name was more commonly used. The Army never really got its act together where dive-bombers were concerned, viewing them as having a low priority, and like the A-25 Shrike the A-24

Banshee attracted little notice. In January 1941 the Army ordered 78 A-24s which were identical to the SBD-3 except that the folding wing capability and carrier arresting tailhook were deleted. A further 90 Navy machines in the same series were modified for Army use with the deletion of shipboard equipment and were delivered to the USAAF as the SBD-3A ('A' for Army). Later in the war the Army ordered 100 A-24As which were identical to the SBD-4 and an impressive 615 A-24Bs which were identical to the SBD-5.

Production of the Dauntless ended on 22 July 1944 and not many examples were kept flyable after the war ended. A few A-24s lingered long after World War II (and, indeed, long after most other Dauntlesses had been scrapped, the type being one for which few museum examples were saved) and some ended up in the Mexican Air Force. One was employed as a target drone in post-war years with the revised designation QF-24A and another as drone controller, the QF-24B.

Among the relatively few dive-bombers used by the USAAF in World War II was a single-seater, the North American NA-97, designated A-36 Apache by the Army and derived from the NA-73 Mustang fighter which had been developed originally for the RAF; the prototype NA-73X made its first flight on 26 October 1940. The Apache, which was also sometimes known as the Invader (not to be confused with the Douglas A-26, which carried the name officially), was powered by a 1,325hp Allison V-1719-87 liquid-cooled engine and was armed with six 0.50in (12.7mm) forward-firing wing guns (two of them firing through the engine cowling). Its most distinctive feature was a set of 'barn door' wing dive brakes, although these eventually proved impractical and were wired up to be inoperative. The first A-36A was delivered in September 1942 and some 500 were ordered.

A few A-36 Apaches reached the combat zone in Sicily and southern Italy and had some success demonstrating themselves as an American equivalent (albeit smaller and faster) of the locally prevalent Luftwaffe Stuka. The first unit to employ the type, the 27th Bomb Group (Dive) operating at Pantelleria, inflicted a considerable amount of damage on German vehicles and convoys. Its six guns were calibrated to give a 100ft (30m) cone of fire at about 300 yards (290m).

The pilot of an A-36 launched his attack by boring down at almost the full vertical and unleashing gunfire and bombs at the same time. As with the Dauntless, this was an exceedingly aggressive way of fighting and was not for the faint of heart. Like the RAF's early Mustang fighters, the A-36 was powered

by the low-altitude rated Allison engine, but as soon as this superlative design had been re-engined with the Rolls-Royce Merlin, it became one of the best fighters of the war. The P-51 Mustang in its later versions carried far more fuel than most fighters and was eventually able to escort bombers to Berlin.

Why, one now wonders, did the Army keep its A-24 Dauntless and A-25 Shrike aeroplanes in the rear areas? With the exception of the Vultee Vengeance, another aircraft which externally had a superficial resemblance to the Dauntless, there was no other Army dive-bomber. The reason seems to be that other missions had greater priority. In the naval context, a dive-bomber could go hurtling down at an enemy warship and could lay its bomb straight down the vessel's smoke stack – as, indeed, the Dauntless did, again and again – but in the land war twin-engined light and medium bombers seemed to be in greater demand.

As for the Vultee V-72 (A-31 and A-35) Vengeance, it may be merciful to say little about an aircraft that achieved little in USAAF service or elsewhere, with one notable exception: in Burma the RAF operated four squadrons of Vengeances (Nos 45, 82, 84 and 110) against pinpoint jungle targets with outstanding success, and very low losses. Manufactured by both Northrop and Vultee (the latter firm having insufficient resources to mass-produce its own design), the type was employed in British service as the Vengeance I, II, III and IV. The aircraft served in US Army colours as the A-31 (300 ordered), A-35A (99 built) and A-35B (831 built, a figure which includes British deliveries). Powered by a 1,700hp Wright R-2600-13 Cyclone radial, the Vengeance was capable of 279mph (449km/h) and carried up to 2,000lb (907kg) of bombs. A sole XA-31B and five XA-31Cs were used to test the airframe with different engines, but no significant improvement resulted.

The Vengeance had a wing span of 48ft (14.63m), length of 39ft 9in (12.12m), height of 15ft 4in (4.67m), and wing area of 332sq ft (30.84m$^2$), making it virtually the same size as the Curtiss Helldiver.

The best that can be said for the Vengeance is that the nickname 'Beast' had already been taken and could not therefore be applied to it. About 340 British-contract Vengeances were supplied to the Royal Australian Air Force and served in Nos 12, 21, 23 and 24 Squadrons, RAAF, with whom they were not very popular; Australia, like the US Marine Corps, was often forced to take whatever aircraft it could get. The fact that the Vengeance was never seriously examined by the US Navy, the principal user of dive-bombers, may be revealing in itself. To

Silhouetted by fading sunlight on 6 July 1944, SB2C Helldivers return to carriers from a bombing strike on Chichi-jima, the same island where torpedo-bomber pilot George Bush was shot down and rescued. Helldivers flew alongside Dauntlesses, Avengers and other carrier-based aircraft. (USN)

paraphrase one pilot, 'It didn't have it, it wasn't going to get it, and we didn't need the airplane.'

The idea of an Army Air Corps dive-bomber (now called a 'strafer', late in the war) had one last gasp with the Vultee XA-41 which was ordered on 10 November 1942 after two competing designs, the Kaiser-Fleet-wings XA-39 and Curtiss XA-40, failed to reach the mock-up stage. Two XA-41s were ordered but only one (43-35124) was delivered – very slowly.

The XA-41 was a massive machine by any standard. Wing span was 54ft (16.45m) and wing area 540sq ft. The bulky fuselage was 48ft 8in (14.83m) in length and height of the aircraft was 14ft 6in (4.41m). Maximum all-up weight was no less than 26,500lb (12,020kg). The machine was de-signed to carry four 37mm cannon plus four 0.30in (7.62mm) machine-guns, all in the fixed forward-firing position in the wings. The XA-41 also had a massive internal bomb bay capable of taking four 1,600lb (725kg) bombs or a torpedo. Power for this monstrous collection of metal and rivets was pro-vided by a single example of the biggest engine then available, the 4,000hp Pratt & Whitney XR-4360-9 radial. This was still very much an experimental powerplant and would remain so until the renamed company, Consolidated Vultee or Convair, employed six of them aboard the post-war B-36 bomber!

Actual construction of the XA-41 took so long, during which time the war changed so much, that little purpose could have remained even in painting markings on it, let alone rolling it out of the hangar. But fly it did, on 11 February 1944 with chief test pilot Frank Davis at the controls.

According to Dustin W. Carter, who was with the company at the time:

'Davis still recalls what a delightful airplane the XA-41 was to fly. The airplane exceeded its total performance envelope – faster top speed, lower handling speed, better climb, etc. Also the airplane was completed some 400lb [181kg] under its design spec weight. It was finished two weeks ahead of its scheduled roll-out date.

'The airplane was easy to fly and was flown often, not only by Davis but by a host of visiting Air Corps officers. The airplane was taken to Eglin Field [Florida] for combat evaluation and was flown by returned combat pilots. Their opinion was high praise but the European war was winding down and the Pacific war required too much over-water flying. The combat pilots opted for the new two-engine [Douglas] A-26 [Invader]. Davis then took [the XA-41] over to Pax River for the Navy to fly. Their evaluation was high praise but they already had two similar machines on order.' Clearly those who were in attendance saw the XA-41 as a hopeful design, but events had passed it by.

Also passed by, as far as the prospects of making effective use of any Dauntless-like aircraft, was the US Army. In the end none of the Army's dive-bomber types – A-24 Dauntless, A-25 Shrike, A-31 and A-35 Vengeance, A-36 Apache, and Vultee XA-41 – made very much difference in the overall scheme of things. The American dive-bomber was the Dauntless and its place was the Pacific war.

What little there is to say about the US Army's employment of the Dauntless can be brief enough. A-24s served with the 27th Bomb Group in New Guinea and were flown by very courageous men on missions which had little impact on the Japanese. Others served with the 531st Fighter-Bomber Group at Makin shortly after the bloody invasion of Tarawa, one of the island-hopping operations which brought American men – and airfields – closer to Japan's homeland. For some unknown reason, although the rear-seat gunner was extremely effective in Navy Dauntlesses, he proved to be less so in the Army. Where one Navy gunner actually exceeded ace status by shooting down seven Japanese Zeros in two days, no Army crewman fared comparably. It is possible that the Army crews flying the A-24 were less well trained than their nautical counterparts in the SBD.

## British Dauntlesses

No one seems to know why Britain belatedly acquired nine Dauntlesses towards the end of the war, when the outcome of the conflict was no longer in doubt and newer aircraft types had been developed and placed in service. Long after they had ceased to represent the state of the art, the SBD-5s in British roundels were given the name Dauntless DB. Mk. I.

Tested at Farnborough in about October 1944 and flown against the Curtiss Helldiver and Vultee Vengeance, the anglicized Dauntless seemed to have nothing in particular to recommend it at this late juncture. (By now Allied aircraft were ranging over Europe, deterred more perhaps by the awful weather than the Luftwaffe, although flak remained a frightening problem; the Nazis' last gasp, the Battle of the Bulge, was looming). Nevertheless, British pilots seemed concerned that the Dauntless was highly vulnerable to enemy fighters.

Joining the ranks of foreign users, the Royal New Zealand Air Force took delivery of eighteen Dauntlesses from US Marine Corps inventory in July 1943, these SBD-3 aeroplanes being assigned to No 25 Squadron, RNZAF. This number was later bolstered by twenty-seven SBD-4s and twenty-three SBD-5s and the New Zealand pilots fought at Bougainville and other Pacific outposts.

France also acquired Dauntlesses for use by her naval air arm, the Aéronavale, which operated the type at Agadir, Morocco, and at Vannes in late 1944 with Flottilles 3F and Flottille 4F. After the liberation of Paris, some French Navy Dauntlesses joined the Allied armada which attacked German pockets of resistance along France's Atlantic coast. A few Dauntlesses remained in French service as trainers at Meknès, Morocco, as late as 1952.

Perhaps the last outpost of the Dauntless was Mexico, where a few examples of the Douglas scout bomber survived well into the 1950s in both military and civil livery.

## Dauntless Survivors

It seems a shame that so few examples of the famous aircraft which served so vitally in the Pacific are available to be seen today. The US Navy Air Museum at Pensacola has an ex-Army A-24 Dauntless, serial 42-60817, restored to represent the Navy dive-bomber. Visitors to the US Marine Corps Museum at Quantico, Virginia, can feast their eyes on an especially well restored example of the Dauntless in Second World War markings. This display aircraft, too, is actually an Army A-24B (serial 42-54582) but

Escort carrier with deck crammed full of Dauntlesses. (USN)

has been refurbished to represent a Marine veteran of the Pacific War.

The only known Navy Dauntless survivor still in airworthy condition is the SBD-5, bureau number 54532, belonging to the Confederate Air Force's 'Ghost Squadron' at Harlingen, Texas. As of late 1988, this aircraft had not been observed on the air show circuit for some time and its exact status was unclear. Thousands of soldiers and sailors heard the sound of the Cyclone-powered Dauntless roaring overhead during the war and it will be a pity if no example of this historic warplane remains available to be appreciated by future generations.

# B-25 Mitchell

The essential shape of the North American B-25 Mitchell, with variations in nose configuration and armament, was seen in every combat theatre. Glass-nosed B-25J-1-NC Mitchell 43-27729 of the 488th Bomb Squadron, 340th Bomb Group – part of the Twelfth Air Force – lets down for a landing on the island of Corsica in March 1944. (via Norman Taylor)

**N**orth American Aviation Inc, head-quartered at Inglewood, California, does not usually come to mind as a manufacturer of bombers. The company's P-51 Mustang fighter became one of a handful of immortals in aviation, but not many remember that the firm leapt into the development of medium-range, twin-engined bombers on the eve of World War II. It was not an easy step to take, for North American had no previous experience with twins, with bombers, or (at the beginning) with high-performance warplanes.

Much of the credit for North American's inventiveness should go to two key figures in the company, Lee Atwood and Ray Rice, who led the design team for the firm's entry into the field. Atwood, who is still with us, began his career with Donald Douglas in the design of the DC-1 transport. He came to North American Aviation and teamed up with J.H. ('Dutch') Kindelberger. The pair were responsible for the BT-9 trainer which later became the AT-6, for the P-51, B-25 and, later, the F-86. Described as a true gentleman by those who know him, Atwood remembers the design of the B-25 Mitchell as a success

which came after the company's earlier, inconclusive work with twin-engined bombers.

The company's little-known XB-21 and XB-28 have been swept handily into the dustbin of history (see pages 113 and 115) but the North American B-25 Mitchell is better remembered, not least because it flew the first offensive American mission against Tokyo. Named in honour of the fearless US Army Air Corps general who was court-martialled in 1924 for his tiresome (to officialdom) championing of air power, the Mitchell is almost certainly the best-known of the wartime bombers which did not have four engines – and the most numerous. It is also a bomber with a friendly constituency, having never been seriously accused of being difficult to fly, handle, or maintain. The Mitchell seems almost to evoke a kind of sweetness from those who flew her.

In 1938 the Army Air Corps was having difficulty funding several aircraft projects it considered essential for the immediate future, but President Franklin D. Roosevelt persuaded Congress to cough up finances and a long-standing requirement for a twin-engined bomber was resurrected. During those lean pre-war years North American had used its own resources to fund development of a bomber it called the NA-40.

The unorthodox and ungainly NA-40 was a three-seat, twin-engined, shoulder-wing bomber with tricycle landing gear and a distinctive 'greenhouse' canopy for its tandem pilot and co-pilot. It looked like a rather uncomfortable collection of iron and was in fact both less graceful and less friendly than the Mitchell which followed. Everything about it spelled difficulty, including a rather awkward crew entrance through a heavy metal door at the nose. The NA-40 was intended to be powered by two 1,100hp Pratt & Whitney R-1830 Twin Wasp radial engines.

When it took to the air on 10 February 1939 with Paul Balfour at the controls, the NA-40, also known as the NA-40-1, was far ahead of competing designs. No one realized yet that many future bombers would have high wings and nosewheels. The NA-40 was well ahead of the game, but seriously underpowered.

## Engine Change

Suitable changes were ordered and with the new company designation NA-40B, the prototype went to Wright Field, Ohio, in March 1939 after conversion to two 1,350hp Wright R-2600-A71 Cyclone engines.

In this pre-war era there was still no US four-engined bomber in widespread use – although Russia had several hundred and the French a few – so the attractive, natural metal NA-40B (also known

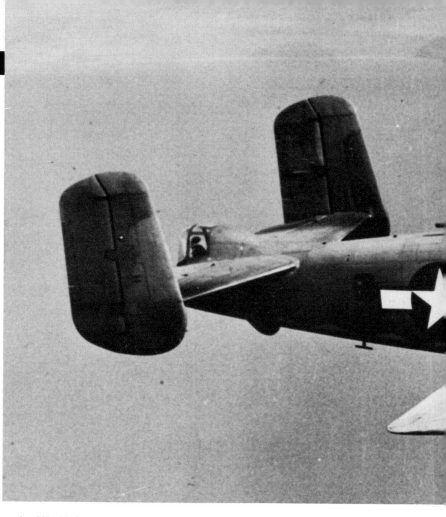

as the NA-40-2 and referred to in company records as aircraft 40-1052) must have impressed onlookers as being very close to the biggest and best that American industry could produce. In tests at Wright Field, the new North American bomber attained a maximum speed of 285mph.

As is so often case, early enthusiasm was dimmed by a crash. Undergoing attack bomber test flights under Major Younger Pitts, the NA-40B was lost in an accident at Wright Field just two weeks after its arrival. Still, the new bomber had been flown enough for test pilots to have a very favourable impression and North American was authorized to continue development.

As North American engineers went to work to improve their design – the new version now being known to the company as the NA-62 – they shifted the high-mounted wing to mid-fuselage, widened the fuselage to increase bomb load, and reconfigured the fuselage contours so that the cockpit was flush with the upper line. The manufacturer had fairly ambitious plans to export the new aircraft, allotted the service designation B-25. The end of the 'greenhouse' brought about a major change in the external appearance of the aircraft, but from this point onward (except for wing dihedral), the essential configuration of the B-25 had been decided upon.

The ubiquitous Mitchell quickly appeared in US Navy and Marine colours. North American PBJ-1 Mitchell (bureau number 35094) on a test flight along the Chesapeake Bay near NAS Patuxent River, Maryland, on 28 February 1944. (via Jim Sullivan)

Never previously published, a privately taken view of North American B-25C Mitchell numbered '36', in desert camouflage. The aircraft belongs to the 434th Bomb Squadron, 12th Bomb Group, and is flying over North Africa's Western Desert in November 1942. (via Norman Taylor)

## Operational Mitchell

On 20 September 1939 North American received a $11.7 million contract for 184 aircraft in the B-25 Mitchell series. The first machine was a static test airframe, completed in July 1940, and the first flight by a production B-25 (40-2165) took place on 19 August 1940 with Vance Breese as pilot.

The B-25 Mitchell was a remarkable aircraft and early tests showed that it had a remarkable performance. Unfortunately, the tests also showed that the B-25 suffered from directional instability. The problem seemed to be caused by wing dihedral. This was corrected by altering the outer wing panels so that they had no dihedral at all. The B-25 weighed in at 27,310lb (12,388kg), or some 7,800lb (3,538kg) more than the high-wing NA-40. The first nine B-25s with excessive dihedral (40-2165 to 40-2173) were followed by fifteen B-25s with the straight outer wings, although no change was made in the designation.

The initial response from pilots and crews was almost overwhelming. Although it never acquired the reputation of being 'hot' or difficult to handle that dogged the Martin B-26 Marauder, the B-25 Mitchell was in fact a very formidable machine, and although it could not outrun fighters, it could often outfight them. The Mitchell was a thrill to fly.

The B-25 bomber which entered service with Lt. Col. Walter R. Peck's 17th Bomb Group at McChord Field, Washington, in 1941 had a five-man crew with pilot and co-pilot seated side-by-side, the crew chief behind them, the bombardier located in the nose and armed with a 0.30in (7.62mm) gun, and the tail gunner with a single 0.50in (12.7mm) machine-gun in a bubble-like rear fuselage mounting. The 17th Bomb Group, incidentally, was credited with the sinking of a Japanese submarine by a B-25 on Christmas Eve 1941.

The story of the submarine sinking, while details seem a bit questionable with the passage of time, is illustrative of the courage and ingenuity that characterized wartime bomber crews. Pilot Brick Holstrom of the 17th Group's 95th Bomb Squadron happened upon the submarine unexpectedly and pressed home the attack. Bombardier George Hammond had forgotten to take off a pitot tube cover which would enable him to use his bombsight, so he used his foot to aim his bomb load, hitting the conning tower of the Japanese submarine squarely. A few months later, pilot Holstrom joined a group being put together by Jimmy Doolittle for reasons which, at the time, were unknown.

**Above: Mitchells in the Marine Corps. A formation of Marine PBJ-1 bombers makes its way through South Pacific skies on a bombing mission on 28 March 1944. In some Marine units the Mitchell was employed virtually as a fighter. (via Jim Sullivan)**

**Top right: Operating at low level, a North American PBJ-1 Mitchell of the US Marine Corps flies over a Pacific island in 1944. (via Jim Sullivan)**

**Right: In tests at Wright Field, Ohio, apparently in 1943, a B-25 Mitchell gets boosted aloft by rocket units under the wings. The rockets were specially developed for aircraft with heavy loads operating from short runways, and these tests were run by the US Army Air Forces Materiel Command from 1940 onwards. The B-25, however, was no more difficult to get off the ground than most other aircraft types in service during the period. (USAF)**

Long after war's end, Columbus, Ohio-built North American B-25J Mitchell 44-86727 was painted in US Marine Corps markings to represent a maritime PBJ-1 Mitchell, and is now on display at Quantico, Virginia. In fact, neither the B-25J nor PBJ-1 were built with the solid nose on this aircraft (nor with the antenna in front of the windscreen), but post-war Mitchells underwent numerous changes before this machine was rolled out for display in the late 1970s. (USMC)

Ordnance men use old-fashioned muscle power to position the payload of a B-25 Mitchell parked and 'tarped' (its guns covered with tarpaulin) on an airstrip of pierced steel planking (PSP) somewhere in the battle zone. (via Dave Ostrowski)

The 17th Bomb Group ended up at Barksdale Field near Shreveport, Louisiana, and was only the first of many units to operate the B-25 effectively on coastal anti-submarine patrols.

For the more intense fighting taking place in Europe, the fast and potent B-25 Mitchell was not well enough armed. A partial answer was the B-25A model, alias NA-62A, which first flew on 25 February 1941 (aircraft 40-2189) with Edward W. Virgin as pilot. Some forty of this model rolled from the Inglewood production line with seal-sealing fuel tanks, improved armour, and other minor improvements, but still with a single tail-gunner. To make the modifications it was necessary to reduce fuel capacity by 246 US gallons, thereby reducing the bomber's range by a hefty 750 miles (1,200km). Weight went up slightly, speed and service ceiling went down slightly.

The original 1939 production order was fulfilled with the delivery of 120 aircraft in the B-25B series (one of which, 40-2243, crashed just after roll-out and had to be written off). With the B-25B a genuine effort was made to improve defensive firepower for the kind of intense fighting expected in Europe.

The B-25B version was stripped of machine-guns except for the single barrel mounted in the bombardier's nose compartment. The tail gun position was reduced in size, resulting in a reduction in fuselage length of 1ft 2in. Leaving only an unarmed, glazed observer's position at the extreme tail, Bendix electrically operated turrets with two 0.50in (12.7mm) guns each were installed in the fuselage in dorsal and ventral positions. The ventral or belly turret was fully retractable and was operated by a gunner who stooped over a periscope gunsight, a rather impractical and uncomfortable arrangement. Power turrets were still new to the Americans at this juncture and there were other technical and practical problems, but the B-25B arrangement worked.

The B-25B version took part in the audacious raid on the Japanese capital mounted by Lt Col James H. Doolittle and his 'Tokyo Raiders'. A well-known airman who had won the Schneider Trophy Race in 1925 and who went on to become commander of the 8th, 12th and 15th Air Forces, Jimmy Doolittle fielded sixteen B-25Bs modified to carry 1,141 US gallons of fuel, nearly twice the standard load. Ventral turrets and Norden bombsights were removed and wooden guns were fitted in the tail to deceive the Japanese.

After secret practice rehearsals at Hurlburt Field, Florida, Doolittle and his colleagues were taken to within 800 miles (1,290km) of the Japanese main island of Honshu aboard the carrier USS Hornet (CV-8). At this distance on 18 April 1942, sooner than planned because Hornet had been spotted by Japanese patrol vessels, the bombers were unlashed from their tie-down points on the flight deck and launched – the B-25B thus becoming the heaviest aircraft ever launched from a carrier at that time.

Doolittle led his modest but determined force in low-level strikes on Tokyo, Yokohama, Nagoya, and Kobe. The raids struck a chord with the American public and persuaded the populace that it was possible to strike back at an enemy who, until then, had seemed invincible. While the actual destruction of military targets was marginal, the effect upon morale was enormous. Doolittle received the Medal of Honor for planning and leading the audacious mission.

The pilots and aircraft on the Doolittle raid were: Lt-Col James H. Doolittle, aircraft 40-2344; Lt Travis Hoover, 40-2292; Lt Robert M. Gray, 40-2270; Lt Everett W. Holstrom, 40-2282; Capt David M. Jones, 40-2283; Lt Dean E. Hallmark, 40-2298; Lt Ted W. Lawson, 40-2261; Capt Edward J. York, 40-2242; Lt Harold F. Watson, 40-2303; Lt Richard O. Joyce, 40-2250; Capt C. Ross Greening, 40-2249; Lt William M. Bower, 40-2278; Lt Edgar E. McElroy, 40-2247; Maj John A. Hilger, 40-2297; Lt Donald G. Smith, 40-2267; Lt William G. Farrow, 40-2268.

Many of the Mitchells failed to find their pre-arranged landing fields in China and several crews fell into enemy hands. Two of the men were executed by firing squad by vindictive Japanese; others were imprisoned for a period. Lawson wrote of the raid in a remarkable book, Thirty Seconds Over Tokyo, which was a best-seller during the war.

Damage was slight from the Doolittle raid but the psychological uplift was real, and the aircraft involved in the mission attained almost instant fame.

## B-25C/D Models

The next version of the Mitchell was the B-25C, delivered from January 1942 onwards and characterized by extensive redesign of small details. The first of these (company designation NA-82) was aeroplane 41-12434 which made its initial flight on 9 November 1941 piloted by the ubiquitous Virgin. In fact, the B-25C and B-25D were identical but were manufactured in different locations, the former in Inglewood, the latter at a newer plant in Kansas City. The first B-25D (company NA-87), serial 41-29648, made its maiden flight in Kansas on 3 January 1942. 1,619 B-25Cs and 3,990 B-25Ds were built.

The B-25C/D was powered by 1,700hp Wright R-2600-13 engines with Holly carburettors and had a 24-volt electrical system, a removable bomb bay fuel

Servicing of most World War II bombers meant climbing on, crawling under, or otherwise contorting in order to reach access doors, control surfaces, or fuel receptacles. At the manufacturer's Los Angeles plant, seven pairs of legs belong to men performing some unknown task in the bomb bay of an early B-25 Mitchell, while a single ground crewman adds engine oil using the receptacle at the top of the wing. (North American)

tank, larger wing fuel tanks, and a de-icer system. The auto-pilot retrofitted on Doolittle raid aircraft became standard.

The RAF took delivery of more than 500 B-25C/ Ds and designated them Mitchell II, the Mitchell I having been the B-25B version (23 supplied). The bombers equipped the RAF's Nos 98, 180, 226, 305 (Polish), 320 (Dutch) and 342 (Free French) Squadrons and were employed almost exclusively in the European theatre. The Dutch Army in the Netherlands East Indies placed an order for 162 B-25C Mitchells in June 1941 but none of these could be delivered before the islands fell. Many of this batch were diverted to Australia where in mid-1942 No 18 (NEI) Squadron was formed by Dutch aircrew on Mitchells, the first Dutch unit created within the RAAF. Later the Australians used Dutch Mitchells in their own No 2 Squadron. 182 B-25Cs, and 688 B-25Ds (including eight of the former lost at sea in transit) were turned over to the Soviet Union. 167 B-25C and 371 B-25D bombers were delivered to the British. Twenty-nine were delivered to Brazil and four more went to the Royal Canadian Air Force.

The XB-25E and XB-25F were converted B-25Cs, one each, with (respectively) hot air de-icers and thermal de-icers. Company records show that the XB-25E (company NA-94) in the form of aircraft 42-32281 took to the air on 4 February 1944 with Joseph Barton as pilot. Both 'E' and 'F' models were converted in early 1942 and it is assumed that both airframes were involved in development work for the B-25C/D series.

As the Mitchell bomber went into service and began to draw blood, field modifications were not uncommon. The USAAF's 345th Bomb Group in the Pacific introduced some aircraft which were modified for a single heavy nose gun or a nose full of forward-firing guns long before similarly equipped Mitchells began to come off the factory production line. Lt Col Paul ('Pappy') Gunn and North American technical representative Jack Fox oversaw the modifications which in time rigged the nose of the Mitchell with as many as a dozen guns. Early in its career it was quite evident that, although the Mitchell had not been designed with strafing in mind, it was in fact an excellent strafer.

It was, in fact, the versatility of the Mitchell that earned the aeroplane a place as one of the key bombers of the war. Although its principal role was always medium-bombing, the Mitchell was also used for transport, reconnaissance, patrol and training. The Mitchell's fuselage, although hardly spacious, was big enough for all sorts of gear to be stuffed into it, and USAAF officers took advantage of every opportunity to put the design to full use.

B-25D-NC Mitchell 41-30192 makes a low-level pass. Appearance of 'last three' on nose is unusual. (via Dave Ostrowski)

Drawing on field experience, the XB-25G Mitchell prototype was developed – a standard B-25C removed from Army inventory and fitted with a standard 75mm field gun in the nose, reflecting the widespread feeling that the Mitchell was both a strafer and a weapons-carrier.

This was followed by the production B-25G. It had been determined that the very large and heavy M4 75mm cannon (9ft 6in long, weighing 900lb) could be carried by the Mitchell if space were made in the crew crawlway and the navigator's position were converted to that of a 'cannoneer'. The production B-25G, of which an impressive 405 were manufactured, carried this M4 75mm gun with twenty-one 15lb (6.81kg) shells.

Loaded by hand, the 75mm gun on the B-25G could rarely get off more than three or four shells in a single firing pass. In combat, the gun proved surprisingly accurate but its slow rate of fire prevented the Mitchell crew from taking evasive action while on the attack. Still, the weapon was remarkably successful in low-level anti-shipping strikes against Japanese merchantmen, and even destroyers proved vulnerable to the 75mm-equipped Mitchells. Two were sent to Britain for evaluation but none was ordered by the RAF.

Operating in the Pacific 'island-hopping' campaign before there could be any assurance of the outcome of the war, the B-25G provided more than its share of challenge to men who flew the cannon-nosed Mitchell from remote places such as Majuro, Makin and Saipan. Tropical weather, which included sudden, violent thunderstorms and sea squalls, could at times be as demanding as the Japanese. Robert G. Lorio, who flew the B-25G with the 41st Bomb Group, found the 75mm cannon frustrating to use but the B-25G Mitchell otherwise very forgiving. 'The crew accommodations were actually spacious, even after they stuffed that cannon in the nose. The aircraft was relatively easy to fly and could be steady as a rock if you had her settled and properly trimmed,'

Its crew reduced from five to four, the B-25G was generally regarded as a success but it remained clear that an improved Mitchell with a cannon was needed.

## Enter the B-25H

The B-25H represented a co-ordinated effort by manufacturer, service-test people, and the operational users of the Mitchell to refine and finalize the 75mm nose cannon configuration. It had been felt all along that reduction of the crew to four in the 'G' model had been unwise, so the B-25H restored a crew size of five.

The B-25H incorporated a newer and better 75mm cannon, the T13E1, positioned (as on the B-25G) off-centre and firing from the lower left side of the nose. The B-25H also carried four 0.50in (12.7mm) machine-guns mounted in the solid nose, and four more in 'packs' mounted flush on the side of the fuselage, giving a total of nine forward-firing guns. a figure later raised to fourteen with some field modifications. No one seems to have dubbed the B-25H 'the flying tank', but with armament similar to that of the M4 Sherman tank of the period the nickname would have been apt.

The B-25H (company model NA-98) flew for the first time on 31 July 1943, the aircraft being 43-4105 with a crew of Chilton and Talman aboard. A B-25H development, dubbed model NA-98X by the manufacturer, had R-2800 engines and flew on 1 April 1944 (aircraft 43-4406) with the crew of Barton and Ferren. Before production of the 'H' model was terminated, an even 1,000 B-25Hs rolled off the production line.

A typical Pacific combat mission with the nose gun-equipped Mitchell was flown by Fourteenth Air Force pilot Lieutenant Bob Pettingell when he and his wingmen took off from a base in south China and flew down to Hainan Island to harry and interdict the Japanese. The two Mitchells were skimming over wavecaps at low level with Hainan Island taking shape to their starboard when they were ambushed by ten Japanese fighters, apparently Nakajima Ki-44 'Oscars'.

With enemy fighters above and a solid wall of ocean below, Pettingell had no room to manoeuvre. He saw two of the 'Oscars' peeling off to come at him in a well co-ordinated attack. One came in high from the side in a beam attack. The other veered around

to assault the Mitchell from the front. The Japanese fighter pilots had calculated a way of splitting up the defensive firepower of the Mitchell.

Pettingell understood what they were up to, instructed his upper turret gunner to take on the beam attacker, and threw his Mitchell around like a fighter to go head-on towards the attacker boring at him from the front. Pettingell fired his nose guns – not the 75mm cannon this time, but the 0.50in (12.7mm) machine-guns arrayed around it – and had the satisfaction of seeing his bullets sparkle against the 'Oscar's' fuselage. A gush of black smoke spewed back from the fighter and it exploded. At the same time, the top turret gunner put several bursts into the other 'Oscar' and watched him erupt into smoke and crash into the sea. Pettingell pressed on with his original mission, proclaiming to the crew, 'We got 'em!'

## The J Model

The most important version of the Mitchell bomber and the most widely used was the B-25J. The B-25J (manufacturer's model NA-108) took to the air for the first time at Kansas City on 3 March 1944, aircraft 43-3870 being piloted by Joe Barton. It was a newer, cleaner Mitchell and it was the version that became most familiar to spotters everywhere.

The B-25J returned to the glazed bombardier nose (the 75mm cannon being deleted) and had one or two fixed and one flexible nose gun. Its crew was increased to six. Among the no fewer than 4,318 B-25J Mitchells delivered, some eight hundred were built with a solid nose and eight 0.50in (12.7mm) guns.

The RAF applied the name Mitchell III to the 314 examples of the B-25J it received, most of which

Los Angeles-built B-25H Mitchell 43-5099, armed with a 75mm cannon and eight forward-firing machine-guns, flies over the sea during a proving flight. An even thousand of these 'H' models were built, of which 248 examples were transferred to the US Navy as the PBJ-1H. The Mitchell was an ideal platform for a heavy armament of forward-aiming firepower. (North American)

This example of the B-25 Mitchell's forward-firing armament is one on which it was not possible to locate any information. Apart from the four 0.50in (12.7mm) forward-firing machine-guns, this Mitchell has three tubes, two of them embedded in the nose, the third slung alongside, which look rather like the standard World War II 3.5in bazooka, or rocket-launcher. This armament combination is located where a 75mm cannon should appear in B-25G and B-25H models. (via David Ostrowski)

were assigned to the 2nd Tactical Air Force. A similar number of B-25Js went to the Soviet Union. Among the unsung heroes of the war were the few brave men who ferried B-25Js and other types to the Russians via a number of routes as farflung as Alaska and Iran, often landing to refuel in ill-equipped locations and struggling onward in difficult weather.

## Dimensions

To use the B-25J as a representative Mitchell, the aircraft had a wing span of 67ft 7in (20.6m). Length was 51ft (15.54m) and height 15ft 9in (4.80m).

Empty, the B-25 Mitchell tipped the scales at 21,100lb (9,580kg) in combat state. Maximum loaded weight was around 35,000lb (15,876kg), although missions were flown at 41,800lb (18,960kg).

Powered by two 1,850hp Wright R-2600-29 Double Cyclone 14-cylinder two-row radial engines, the Mitchell could attain a maximum speed of 275mph (443km/h), climb at the rate of 1,100ft (338m) per minute, had a service ceiling of 24,000ft (7,315m) and range of 1,500 miles (2,414km).

All performance figures were of course subject to variation depending upon where, when, temperature, the aggressiveness of aircrews, and ninety-five other factors. Just as it was never settled which was the fastest fighter of World War II, so it will never be known which was the fastest US twin-engined bomber, although the Mitchell certainly presented some competition to the Martin B-26 Marauder.

Nevertheless, the Mitchell was the outstanding US medium bomber of the war, principally because it was trouble-free, easily maintained, and easily flown. In Tunisia, Sicily, the Western Pacific and the

Aleutians the B-25 Mitchell proved itself able to accommodate crude working conditions, heat, dust, and Arctic cold. In low-level missions against ships, trucks, and a dozen kinds of enemy installations, the B-25 Mitchell could return safely with its propellers green from the grass it had been flying through.

One pilot who remembers the B-25 Mitchell from operations in Sicily and Italy is former Captain Edward McPherson. On one mission, McPherson and crew were aloft for nearly four hours on what had begun as a routine mission. Battered by a 'near miss' from a German 88mm anti-aircraft shell, their B-25 suffered electrical failure and had one engine badly damaged, although still running. McPherson's tail gunner then discovered four Messerschmitt Me 109 fighters closing on them from dead astern. 'I put the pedal to the metal,' McPherson remembers. 'We had concluded that we could give them a good race

for their money as long as they didn't have an altitude advantage on us.' McPherson outran one Messerschmitt, saw his tail gunner put holes in another, and went on to finish his mission and bomb his target successfully.

## B-25 Transports

An important part of the B-25 Mitchell story concerns six B-25s converted by North American to RB-25 transports, beginning in 1942. In December 1942 the first such aircraft, B-25 40-2165, was fitted with executive accommodation in the rear fuselage and was used by North American to carry its own corporate leaders around the country to visit outposts in the firm's growing empire. Often used by corporate president J. H. ('Dutch') Kindelberger, this RB-25 was referred to as 'Dutch's Airplane' or the

Preparing for their famous raid on Tokyo, James Doolittle's force of B-25B Mitchell bombers is lined up on the flight deck of the aircraft-carrier USS *Hornet* (CV-8) on 18 April 1942. Looking for an early way to attack Japan, US leaders considered using flying-boats such as the PB2Y Coronado or PB2M Mars, before settling on the option of carrier-launched Mitchells. (via Dave Ostrowski)

B-25A Mitchell 41-12823 over California mountains not far from the Los Angeles plant where it was built. (via Dave Ostrowski)

North American's NA-40 bomber design of the pre-war period was the precursor of the B-25 Mitchell, but had a wholly different 'greenhouse' and nose configuration for its crew of five. While the eventual B-25 had similar wings and tail, it was in most respects a new design. The NA-40 carries the civil registration number NX-14221. (via Norman Polmar)

By the time the NA-40B appeared in the immediate pre-war era, the original NA-40 configuration had been dramatically changed and the basic appearance of the B-25 Mitchell was set. Seen at Mines Field (today's Los Angeles International Airport) in natural metal and pre-war markings, the NA-40 has most of the characteristics of the Mitchell which followed. (North American)

Typical of B-25 Mitchells which laboured hard and long in the post-war US Air Force, some of them serving as navigator trainers while others (like this one) were in the livery of the Military Air Transport Service (MATS), this machine (44-30457) was built as a B-25J and now – in November 1957 – appears to be a VB-25J executive transport. (USAF)

Front view of a B-25J Mitchell on the ground at Los Angeles. Note the anti-glare shield on the inboard side of engine cowlings. (North American)

'Whiskey Express'. It served for two and a half years before being written off as a result of a crash at the factory.

A second RB-25 transport was converted for USAAF chief General Henry H. (Hap) Arnold. 40-2166 may have been the serial number of Arnold's ship, although the record is unclear. The aircraft was nicknamed 'L'il Abner' after the popular cartoon character. Arnold, it will be remembered, was in constant motion partly because of his role in moulding the wartime bomber force.

A more advanced Mitchell, RB-25J 43-4030, was converted for General Dwight D. Eisenhower's use and, soon afterwards, General Arnold shifted to RB-25J 44-28945.

RB-25J 44-30047, converted in January 1945, became North American Aviation's second Mitchell executive transport. After the war this aircraft was lost off the California coast in a tragic accident which took the life of Joe Barton, a respected and accomplished company test pilot.

During the post-war period at least two more Mitchells were converted to transports by North American. One of these was B-25J 44-30975 (Navy Bureau No 35848) which became the wholly rebuilt 'Executive Transport' with a different nose profile,

completely redesigned interior, and Convair 240 windshield assembly and instrument panel. With the civil registration N5126N, this aircraft was lost in 1950 with seven key company executives aboard, bringing an end to the manufacturer's involvement with transport Mitchells.

## Reconnaissance Craft

There was also a photo-reconnaissance version of the Mitchell, the F-10. Only ten were acquired, these being converted from B-25D bombers in inventory. The success of field-modified bombers in the reconnaissance role led to development of the F-10, with a trio of cameras in a chin fairing for trimetrogen photography. Defensive armament was removed from the F-10 and additional fuel tanks were installed in the bomb bay. These aircraft went in 1944 to the 11th Photographic Reconnaissance Group with detachments at MacDill Field, Florida, and Bradley Field, Connecticut. So far as can be determined, the F-10 version never served in combat.

It seems probable that at least a couple of the photorecce aeroplanes survived the war to serve the independent USAF as RB-25s (not to be confused with the RB-25 transports previously noted). Throughout the war, of course, other Mitchells were converted to the reconnaissance role in the field.

## Maritime Mitchell

The Mitchell bomber served not only with US Army Air Forces but also with the US Navy and Marine Corps. Naval designations for each of the principal models employed were PBJ-1 (for the B-25B), PBJ-1C (B-25C), PBJ-1D (B-25D), PBJ-1H (B-25H) and PBJ-1J (B-25J), the final tally of naval Mitchell airframes adding up to 706. These 'patrol bombers', as their designation brands them, had different radio equipment, were fitted with radar, and carried depth-charges in lieu of bombs. On occasion they carried different radar and search-lights for night operations and were even employed as night fighters. Some PBJ-1Js carried a distinctive radar set in a tip tank on the starboard wing only.

The first multi-seat combat aircraft flown by the Marine Corps in living memory was the PBJ-1 Mitchell which went to Squadron VMB-413 at Cherry Point, North Carolina, in March 1943. This squadron headed into combat in the Pacific Theatre, arriving at Espiritu Santu in early 1944. Once bombing techniques were perfected (after an early tragedy when two planes with full crews were lost on 22 March 1944), the Mitchell proved highly effective in

Pacific combat. By war's end, the nine squadrons which reached the battle zone had lost in combat a respectably low 26 aircraft, plus nineteen non-combat losses.

One of the more dramatic events involving the PBJ Mitchell was its landing aboard an aircraft-carrier. Just as Doolittle's Raiders had managed with difficulty to take off from a carrier, a task for which the Mitchell had never been designed, so was the Navy able to demonstrate that the big, twin-engined bomber could be brought aboard ship of neccesary. On 15 November 1944 Lt-Cdr H. S. (Syd) Bottomley landed PBJ-1H 35277 aboard the USS *Shangri-la* in tests. Carrier operations with the Mitchell did not have any immediate practical application, but 'lessons learned' were consulted again in post-war years when the Navy developed its fleet of North American Savage shipboard bombers.

During World War II a number of Mitchell bombers with high airframe hours were turned over to stateside training commands to be used for instructional work, primarily as flying classrooms for fledgling bombardiers. Some were used to instruct in BTO (bombing through overcast) techniques at Yuma airfield in Arizona. The designations AT-24A, 'B, 'C and 'D were applied to USAAF training versions of the B-25A, 'B, 'C and 'D. These were not necessarily the same airframes which ended up in the training role in the post-war era (see later) but during the years of the conflict they were critical in preparing aircrews for their mission.

Post-war versions of the B-25 Mitchell performed a variety of roles in the US Air Force, which became an independent service in 1947. These conversions included the TB-25K, TB-25L, TB-25M, and TB-25N. As a trainer for navigators operating from Mather AFB, California, the TB-25 Mitchell served well into the late 1950s when it was replaced by the same manufacturer's T-39 Sabreliner. The Royal Canadian Air Force (RCAF) was one of the more numerous users of the B-25 well into the 1960s. Other Mitchells served in the US Air National Guard or as base 'hacks' at airfields around the country. VJ-Day ended the combat career of the Mitchell, however – except for small wars in Latin America – and none served in Korea or Vietnam.

As with many wartime aircraft types, the B-25 Mitchell became a candidate for second-level foreign air forces as soon as the fighting ended and also appeared in civil livery. The B-25 appeared after the war in air arms as far apart as Taiwan and Peru. Eight appeared on the civil register in Argentina. Some aircraft delivered originally to Nationalist China fell into the hands of the Communist side in mainland China.

In due course, civil Mitchells became executive transports, crop-dusters and fire-bombers, and a few were preserved as 'warbirds' by well-to-do men with a sense of history. Several Mitchells are still flying today and can be seen regularly at air shows.

To exemplify the gun-armed Mitchells, B-25H 43-4108 has been restored for display at the Birchwood Airport Museum in Anchorage, Alaska. A finely preserved glass-nosed Mitchell is B-25J 44-31004, located with the impressive aircraft display that has grown up beside the battleship *Alabama* in Mobile. Another, 44-20444, has been aptly preserved for outdoor display at General Billy Mitchell Field in Milwaukee, Wisconsin. The flying examples have been noted with Challenge Publications, the Confederate Air Force, and other owners. One of the more nicely preserved Mitchells is TB-25N (originally a B-25J) 43-27868 belonging to the Yellow Rose Squadron of the Confederate Air Force in San Antonio, Texas.

## Wartime Operators

There can hardly have been an Allied airfield anywhere during the war which did not see a B-25 Mitchell in operation at one time or another. USAAF Mitchells may have been rare in Britain, but home-based RAF squadrons used Mitchells by the hundred. In places as remote as Chittagong, India, or Adak, Alaska, the Mitchell showed up and soldiered on.

Wartime USAAF units which employed the B-25 Mitchell included the stateside 13th, 17th, 25th, and 309th Bomb Groups, the Mediterranean Theatre's 12th, 310th, 321st and 340th Groups, and the European Theatre's 477th Group (a Hollywood offering entitled 'Hanover Street' notwithstanding, USAAF B-25s did not go into combat from the British Isles).

In the Pacific, units which operated the Mitchell included the 3rd, 38th, 41st, 42nd, 341st and 345th Bomb Groups. Some Mitchell bombers were used to ferry generals and other VIPs around, so B-25s ended up in many other units, not always for the purpose of dropping bombs.

Virtually all the naval PBJ Mitchells, obtained with US Navy funding, went to the Marine Corps. Marine squadrons which eventually used some variant of the Mitchell included VMB-413, -423, -433, -443, -611, -612, -613 and 614. At the Marine Corps Museum at Quantico, Virginia, wartime Marine markings are preserved on B-25J 44-86727, painted to represent a PBJ-1 Mitchell. This aircraft is one of the very best examples available for public viewing and is a great tribute to a great aeroplane.

Another B-25 Mitchell which underwent a post-war change of nose configuration is B-25J 44-86891, seen on 14 January 1980 on its last flight en route to Castle Air Force Base, California, to be placed on display at the Fifteenth Air Force Museum. For many years after World War II there was little interest in the USA in aircraft preservation, but a revival in the 1970s and 1980s resulted in many restorations. (USAF)

In January 1971 all the historic aircraft belonging to the US Air Force Museum at Wright-Patterson AFB, Ohio, were moved from an older location to the museum's present site near Dayton. The move resulted in this highly unusual parade in which the Museum's B-25J Mitchell (43-3374) leads a B-24, P-61 and other types down an Ohio roadway. A remarkable number of B-25 Mitchells have survived into the 1990s, many still in flying condition. (USAF)

# The Lesser-Known Bombers

Today it would be unthinkable. In the late 1930s key decisions about US strategic weaponry were made by a handful of junior officers. Had it not been for Maj Gen Frank Armstrong and Lt Col Robert Olds, there would have been no daylight bomber fleet to pound Nazi Europe in World War II. These men and a few others pioneered the four-engined, high-altitude, long-range bomber and encouraged the vision of the Boeing company which wanted to build it.

Likewise, it took a remarkable industry to design, develop and build the bombers of the Second World War. Every country had brains. Every nationality had its share of brilliant men who could turn a concept into an engineering drawing and later into an aeroplane. Only the United States had people and resources in abundance and could experiment with and develop so many new bomber designs at the very time it was turning out tens of thousands of examples of existing bombers.

Secure behind their own shorelines in the certain knowledge that no one would ever attack their homeland, the Americans designed, developed and built dozens of prototypes for new aircraft. Outclassed by their adversaries at the beginning of the conflict, they commanded the world in quantity and (often) quality by its end. Apart from Britain, no one else seriously attempted to produce four-engined bombers during the war – German, Russian and Italian efforts in this field were limited – yet when a handful of brave US Army Air Corps officers defined the need, an enterprising American industry turned out more than a dozen different designs to choose from.

It was never decreed that there should be four-engined bombers. Yet long before the outbreak of fighting and before the Flying Fortress and Liberator

The progenitor of all big US four-engined bombers to follow, the Boeing XB-15 was virtually a contemporary of the Model 299 which became the B-17 – but was even bigger. During its first flight on 15 October 1937, the XB-15 performed well but kept its landing gear down. The XB-15 was eventually relegated to the transport role but contributed much to the development of the bombers that became operational during the war. (Boeing)

became household names, Boeing developed its remarkable XB-15 bomber as a kind of flying laboratory for the concept.

And what an aeroplane it was! Even in today's post-industrial era, the Boeing Model 294, or XB-15, seems remarkable. Built to satisfy a US Army requirement of 1933 for an aircraft initially designated XBLR-1 (in competition with an unsuccessful Martin design the XB-16, to have been powered by two pusher and four tractor engines!), the Boeing XB-15 was the largest American aircraft ever built when it made its initial flight at Seattle on 15 October 1937.

Wing span was 149ft (only 36ft less than today's B-52). Wing area measured 2,780sq ft. The XB-15 fuselage was 87ft 7in in length, and the height of the aircraft was 18ft 1in. This behemoth weighed a modest 37,709lb when empty but maximum take-off weight rose to an impressive 70,700lb.

So big was the XB-15 (serial number 35-277) that it had tunnels in the wing to permit engine repairs while in flight. So spacious was the bomber that it had bunks and cabinets for a second relief crew. (Crew size was ten men). The XB-15 was one of the first American bombers with gun turrets. It also featured sound-proofed, heated, and ventilated cabins. With all its innovations, the XB-15 was capable of reaching 195mph in level flight. Range was 5,130 miles, service ceiling 19,000ft.

Alas, this first American four-engined bomber was seriously underpowered, there being no adequate engine available in the late 1930s. Its four 1,000hp Pratt & Whitney R-1830-11 Twin Wasp Senior radial engines were responsible for the relatively modest speed and ceiling.

Always a one-off test article for which no production plans ever existed, the XB-15 was flown exhaustively to evaluate bomber concepts. On 30 July 1939 it carried a 31,167lb payload to an altitude of 8,200ft. On 2 August 1939, while carrying a payload of 4,409lb, it remained in the air for no less than 18 hours 40 minutes 47 seconds. Knowledge gained from the XB-15 led to the US Army Air Corps eventually acquiring another aircraft which by 1939 equipped the 49th Bombardment Squadron under Lt Col Olds at Langley AFB, Virginia – the Boeing B-17 Flying Fortress. The first version of the B-17 had actually flown earlier (28 July 1935), but partly because of the early loss of the first prototype, information acquired from the XB-15 flight programme proved valuable to the development of the Fortress.

The contribution of the latter aircraft to the history of weapons and warfare is touched upon in the first chapter. Suffice to say that after World War II had started, the XB-15 took on a new and different role. Fitted with cargo doors, it was operated as a transport and was redesignated XC-105.

In Panama today there exists a mound believed to contain the dismantled remnants of the scrapped XC-105 (former XB-15) which may be in good enough condition to warrant excavation and restoration. A number of history specialists have been searching for a way to muster the resources to save this unusual aviation treasure.

As for the competing XB-16 devised by the Glenn L. Martin Company in Baltimore and placed on order in 1935, this apparently would have been a gargantuan craft powered by no fewer than six 1,100hp Allison V-1710-3 liquid-cooled in-line engines (which, as we shall see with similarly powered versions of production bombers, never succeeded at all as a bomber powerplant), arranged with two pusher and four tractor propellers.

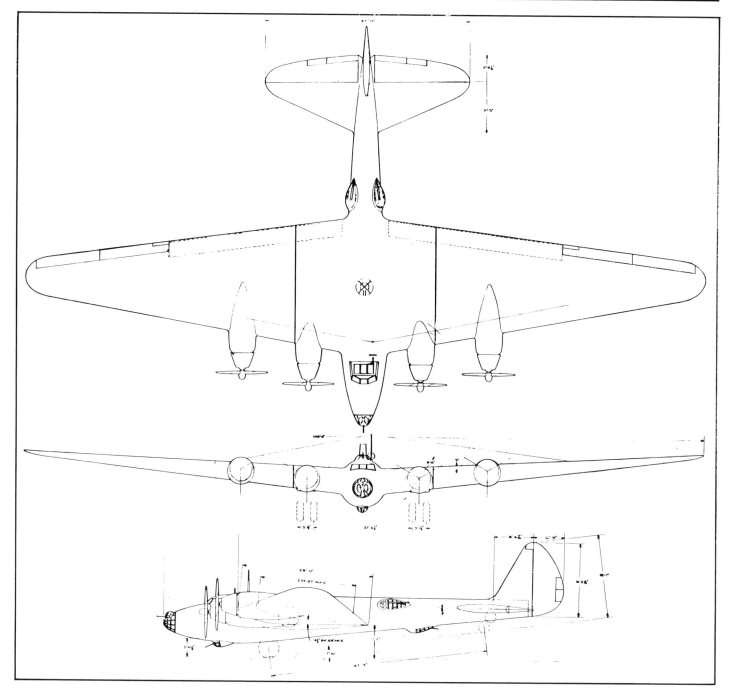

Line drawing of the XB-15.

The XB-16 would have weighed no less than 108,800lb with a wing span of 173ft (roughly the same as today's B-52) and fuselage length of 115ft. The proposal never reached the metal-cutting stage and no XB-16 was actually built.

## Douglas B-18

When the Japanese attacked Pearl Harbor and the Philippines on 7 December 1941, the US Army's standard medium bomber was an obsolescent and ungainly twin-engined craft based on the Douglas

DC-2 transport. The Douglas B-18 bomber, widely named the Bolo but known as the Digby in Canadian service, was scarcely more than a transport with a bomb bay! Although not being widely known or publicized, it did, in fact, enjoy widespread operational service but was neither effective nor popular. The B-18 was nothing more or less than an incredible starting point for a nation which, within three years, built up the most massive bombing force the world had ever seen.

The Douglas DB-1 (Douglas Bomber 1) was put into production as the B-18 to meet US Army Air

Corps requirements (and perhaps as insurance against the failure of the forthcoming B-17 Flying Fortress) in December 1936. Outwardly similar to the company's transport, the B-18 had a wing span of 89ft 6in (27.28m) – some 4ft 6in (1.37m) more than the DC-2 – mated to an entirely new fuselage, deeper than that of the commercial aeroplane, and with a glazed nose position for a bombardier. The latter proved important to film-goers who, in the motion picture 'Bombardier', watched pre-war B-18 crews send a rain of whistling death down on evil foreign aggressors.

Six men comprised the B-18's crew, including a ventral gunner whose weapon was manned from a lower-fuselage tunnel position. The production B-18A was powered by two 1,000hp Wright R-1820-53 Cyclone 9 radial engines. Orders were placed for 133 B-18s and 217 B-18As.

Flying the B-18 was apparently a pleasant enough task, the flight cabin being quite roomy. Although it was a 'taildragger', the pilot had remarkably good visibility when taxi-ing. The crew, in fact, had far more space and greater comfort than does the crew of today's B-52 Stratofortress!

The B-18 was 57ft 10in (17.63m) long with a height of 15ft 2in (4.62m) and a wing area of 965sq ft (89.65m²). Maximum speed was 215mph (346km/h). Defensive armament comprised three 0.30in (7.62mm) machine-guns and the aircraft could carry up to 6,500lb (2,948kg) of bombs.

A handful of B-18As were at Clark Field near Manila when the Japanese launched their 8 December 1941 (west of the international dateline) attack. B-18s of the 5th and 11th Bomb Groups at Wheeler Field, Hawaii, were wiped out when the Japanese launched their attack on Pearl Harbor. It readily became apparent that the B-18 was too slow and too vulnerable for action in a real war, and 1939 was the last fiscal year in which any of the aircraft were ordered.

Followed by a North American BC-1 trainer before the term 'chase plane' was in vogue, a Douglas B-18 Bolo with early nose configuration flies over southern California with its landing gear down. (USAF)

## Wartime Variants

With the outbreak of fighting, the designation B-18B was developed for some 122 aeroplanes which were rigged with special radio equipment and relegated to anti-submarine duties in the Caribbean and South Atlantic. The designation B-18C was assigned to two machines with additional modifications for work against German U-boats. Some aeroplanes stripped of bombing gear were reportedly designated B-18AM and B-18M. A development in the series which would have been powered by two 1,600hp Wright R-2600-3 radial engines was known as the B-22 but was never built. The designation C-58 was given to a further two aircraft converted for use in the transport role.

The Royal Canadian Air Force received twenty B-18As, and named the type Digby. Retrofitted with items of British and Canadian internal equipment, they were issued to No 10 Squadron, RCAF, and began maritime anti-submarine operations in June 1940.

The B-18A cruised at 167mph (269km/h), had a service ceiling of 23,900ft (7,285m) and a range of 1,200 miles (1,931km). It might have enjoyed a more colourful career had its principal competitor, the B-17 Flying Fortress, not proved such a success. But even in pre-war years it was obvious that while the B-17 was destined for immortality, the B-18 was merely going to fade away.

## Douglas B-19

A wholly different kind of aircraft, the B-19 bomber from the same manufacturer was billed as the largest aircraft in the world.

The B-19 was spawned by the same requirement for a 'very heavy' bomber which had also produced the Boeing XB-15. The sole example (later given serial 38-471) was ordered on 29 September 1936, to be powered by four 2,000hp Wright R-3350-5 Cyclone radials. Its main wheels were 8ft in diameter! Delays caused the B-19 to take to the air three years later than originally expected, on 27 June 1941. Had it flown when planned, the mere existence of the B-19 as a mammoth, four-engined, long-range bomber would have been even more impressive than it was – and it was very impressive!

The B-19 introduced the first power-boosted controls on an American bomber, but it is better remembered simply for its size – 212ft (64.61m) wingspan, loaded weight of 780,000lb (353,800kg). In its original form, the B-19 was designed to carry a bomb load of 18,700lb (8,482kg). The crew numbered eleven to eighteen, depending on the mission.

After it became clear that the B-19 would not be ordered into production (there appeared to be no benefit in shifting from mass production of B-17 and B-24), the sole example was re-engined with 2,600hp Allison V-3420-11 double water-cooled powerplants and redesignated XB-19A. In this form it became one of several wartime bombers to test the in-line engines (as our discussion of the Vega XB-38 and Boeing XB-39 will indicate), although no advantage over air-cooled radials was demonstrated.

Seen at Wright Field and other airfields during the war years and for a short time afterwards, the B-19 never ceased to overwhelm observers with its size and bulk. The aircraft was a prodigious aerodynamic and structural achievement, but neither of its powerplants were adequate for its enormous weight. The

Except for its new deeper fuselage, the Douglas B-18A Bolo bomber looked pretty much like the DC-2 transport from which it was derived, which meant that it was cavernous and slow. The anti-glare shield, bright-coloured engine nacelles (red?) and stars and stripes on the tail all add to the silvery glint of natural metal in this 8 August 1940 view – and would attract an enemy fighter if one were in the area. (via Dave Ostrowski)

B-19 tested numerous systems including electrics, hydraulics, armament and bombsights (to say nothing of powerplants) and actually flew for a time after the war before it was thoughtlessly scrapped. Few aircraft in history were so impressive and few were as deserving of being preserved for future generations.

In point of fact, the B-19 may have done more for the war effort than could be expected of a single airframe. Wherever it went on the flight test, travel and display circuit, the great silvery B-19 was testimony to the power and might of the US Army Air Forces. It was billed that way and shown off that way. It was used to promote sales of War Bonds and financial sponsorship of aircraft purchases. It was a symbol at a time when symbols were important and it said to Americans that they were going to win because the seemingly inexhaustible wealth of their industry had finally been geared up for action.

## Boeing XB-20

Another aircraft that would have been most impressive, had it been built, was the Boeing XB-20, an improved version of the giant XB-15. Two were ordered in 1937 under the designation Y1B-20 and were to be powered by four 1,400hp Pratt & Whitney R-2180-5 radials. The Y1B-20 was to be 98ft long with a wing span of 152ft. Details of the external appearance of this design have never been published and construction of the two prototypes was cancelled on the eve of the war.

One of the lesser-known bomber types of the war period was the North American XB-21, a twin-engined craft not dissimilar in appearance to the Douglas B-18 or DC-3. Powered by two super-charged 1,200hp Pratt & Whitney R-2180 Twin Hornet engines, the XB-21 was 61ft in length with a 95ft wing span. It looked like a 'hack', or aircraft designed solely for general purpose duties. The lacklustre XB-21 flew for a brief period during the pre-war years but had little effect on bomber design.

## Douglas B-23

Based on the DC-3 transport (in much the same way that its earlier B-18 bomber was based on the DC-2 transport), the Douglas B-23 Dragon twin-engined bomber appeared in 1939 and was rather sleek and slim considering its origins. It was the classic pre-war bomber. Had the world not hurled itself into a global conflict which saw rapid change, the B-23 might have served in larger numbers and achieved greater longevity.

Because its design was so close to the proven B-18, the first production B-23 Dragon (serial 39-27) was able to fly on 27 July 1939 without being preceded by any experimental prototype. Powered by two 1,600hp Wright R-2600-3 Cyclone 14 engines and capable of a maximum speed of 278mph (447km/h), the B-23 had been built around the notion that if a bomber was fast enough, no forward armament would be necessary. Before long, a generation of Luftwaffe fighter pilots was going to show Fortress and Liberator airmen otherwise.

The US Army Air Corps ordered thirty-eight B-23 Dragons, the final twelve of which were converted to UC-67 transport standard. Compared with previous Douglas twin-engined machines, the B-23 was virtually a new design. Wing span was increased to 92ft (28.04m). The fuselage, 58ft 4¾in (17.80m) in length, was slimmer and aerodynamically more

Left: Another Douglas bomber based on a transport was the B-23 Dragon, which owed its inspiration to the immortal DC-3. An aircraft which would have been adequate had World War II not accelerated the pace of aircraft development, the B-23 ended up serving through the war as a 'hack' and transport. The two aircraft shown in these views were converted to civil executive transports by Hughes Aircraft immediately after the war. (Hughes)

Above: A Douglas B-23 Dragon bomber converted to an executive transport by Hughes after the war. (Hughes)

appealing. The tail unit had a taller fin, reaching a height of 18ft 5½in (5.63m). Wing area was also greater than the DC-2, DC-3 or B-18, reaching 993sq ft (92.25m²). A 'taildragger', the B-23 had retractable landing gear and extended engine nacelles which were faired to cover the tucked-in mainwheels in flight.

Although it looked good, the B-23 Dragon had a disappointing performance. Apart from its unimpressive top speed, the B-23 cruised at 210mph (338km/h), had a service ceiling of 31,700ft (9,662m) and carried a mediocre 4,400lb (1,996kg) of bombs. Douglas engineers and US Army engineers were told in 1940, based on experience from the war then raging in Europe, that a B-23 stretched to the maximum of its development potential would still not measure up to the standard of bombers developed by the belligerent nations.

Like its B-18 predecessor, the B-23 Dragon saw limited service on anti-submarine patrols close to American shores; its wartime record was undramatic. The Dragon was basically a good aeroplane, but not a good bomber, and in the post-war years many were acquired by civil operators for modification as corporate aircraft. Some were converted by Pan American's engineering department and fitted to carry a dozen passengers with a crew of two. Some remained in service for about 30 years.

At least one example of the B-23 Dragon, airworthy today, has a colourful past. Aircraft N747M, which visited the Chino (Calif.) 'Planes of Fame' fly-in 1988 and is owned by Mike Bogue of Oakland, California, had previously served as a personal executive transport for two of the more flamboyant men in aviation, Ed Daly of World Airways and billionaire Howard Hughes. N747M is in superb condition and appears likely to go on flying forever. Remarkably, at least a half-dozen other B-23s are also preserved.

## North American XB-28

Although North American Aviation had no bomber experience when it created the magnificent B-25 Mitchell, the company moved quickly in pre-war years to develop a pressurized, high-altitude offspring of the B-25. With the company designation NA-62, the XB-28 (40-3056) was rolled out in early 1942 in natural metal finish and was camouflaged before it flew. The bomber took to the air on 24 April 1942 with Edward W. Virgin as pilot and one other crewman on board. As it turned out, the rather attractive XB-28 contributed substantially to the knowledge that went into bomber development during the war years.

The XB-28 was powered by two 2,000hp Pratt & Whitney R-2800-11 twin-row, air-cooled 18-cylinder radials driving four-bladed propellers. The bomber had a wingspan of 72ft 7.4in, was 56ft 4½in long, 21ft 11½in high, and had a wing area of 675.9sq ft. It had a maximum speed of 372mph at 25,000ft and a range of 2,040 miles with 600lb of bombs. Maximum gross weight was 39,125lb.

Aircraft 40-3056 was flight-tested rather extensively with its planned operational crew of five. It was one of the first American bombers to feature remote-control gun turrets, three of them, operated by a gunner from the pressurized crew compartment. Its six 0.5in guns, two each in the three turrets, were aimed through a 180deg 'fish-eye' periscope. This arrangement for defensive armament was similar to that eventually adopted for the B-29 Superfortress.

The XB-28 seems to have been promising, but a programme to develop three prototypes never reached fruition. The first aircraft went to Wright Field, Ohio, but after further testing it was stripped of its wings and used as a high-altitude pressurization chamber. A projected second XB-28 (40-3057) was never completed.

The third machine (40-3058), with improved R-2800-27 engines and the new designation XB-28A, made its maiden flight exactly a year after the first, on 24 April 1943, again with Virgin as pilot. The XB-28A was not long for this world, however, and no photograph is known to have survived.

On 4 August 1943 XB-28A 40-3058 was aloft for 'fixed rudder, rate of roll' tests with Bob Chilton as pilot and Roy Ferrin as flight test engineer. After an hour and a half of tests, the aircraft developed a violent tail shake and rudder pedal oscillation while in a dive and Chilton, losing control, determined that it was necessary to hit the silk. Ferrin went aft, forced open the lower hatch, and baled out over the sea a few miles from Balboa, California. Chilton remained aboard for a minute or two and leapt out at 6,000ft. Separated by considerable distance, the men were rescued by civilian boats, one of them manned by a former RAF pilot who had himself been rescued from the English Channel during World War I.

It remains unclear why the second of three XB-28s was never completed. The B-28 might well have made a very effective medium bomber, together with the Mitchells and Marauders that fought in every theatre of the war. But by August 1943 with one airframe reduced to duty as a wingless pressure chamber and the other lying at the bottom of the sea, there was no practical way to continue the XB-28 programme, which was discontinued.

Ed Virgin, who headed the manufacturer's Washington, DC office in the 1950s, always spoke highly of the XB-28 and XB-28A, claiming that they could have hastened the end of the war had they come along earlier. Certainly, flight testing of this machine contributed to knowledge about armament, pressurization, and other aspects of bomber operations which increased in importance when the B-29 came along.

## XB-30 and others

In 1941 the USAAF began work on the XB-30 bomber designed by Lockheed. The Douglas XB-31 was under development at the same time. Both were to have been powered by four 2,200hp Wright R-3350-13 radials. Both were also cancelled very early in the development stage, the Lockheed design surviving long enough for historian James C. Fahey to note that it would have had a wingspan of 123ft and been 104ft 8in long. In later years both these designs re-emerged as cargo aircraft, the Lockheed C-69 Constellation and Douglas C-74 Globemaster, but no prototype of either design was ever built as a bomber.

So much innovation was occurring during the war years that at times it was almost a matter of chance as to which bombers got built and which did not. One aircraft which probably might have made more of a mark, had its competitor not proved so exemplary, was the four-engined Consolidated Model 33, ordered by the USAAF as the B-32 Dominator. The little-publicized B-32 Dominator was built to satisfy the same requirement that led to the B-29 Superfortress. As with its rival, the B-32 began life as the result of a firm order for three prototypes.

In many respects an outgrowth of the same manufacturer's Liberator, the B-32 Dominator took to the air for the first time on 7 September 1942, just two weeks before the first Superfortress. It was a giant aircraft with a variation on the Davis wing, twin tails, and not much in the way of insignia and markings but for horizontal red and white stripes on its distinctive, Liberator-style twin rudder.

The B-32 Dominator was pressurized for high-altitude operations and had remotely controlled gun turrets (both, again, having also been tried in the unsuccessful North American XB-28). From the third B-32 onwards, the twin tail configuration was dispensed with, being replaced by a rather formidable single vertical surface, and re-designed nose turret and windshield details.

Powered by four 2,200hp Wright R-3350-23 Cyclone radial engines, the B-32 was credited with a maximum speed of 357mph (575km/h) at 25,000ft (7,620m). Just a little smaller than the Superfortress

The second prototype Consolidated XB-32 Dominator (41-0142), with the double tail which was discarded in the production aeroplane, flies near the San Diego plant where it was built. The original design also lacked a nose turret which became standard on the operational aircraft. In early tests the XB-32 experienced stability problems but was generally seen as a promising design. (Consolidated/Otto Menge)

Identical to the operational bomber except that it lacks a nose power turret, Consolidated TB-32 Dominator 42-108521 flies near Fort Worth, Texas, where production was transferred from San Diego. The serial number of this aircraft is, itself, an illustration of the awesome power of American industry – the 108,521st airframe ordered in fiscal year 1942 which ended on 30 September 1942, nine months after the US entry into the war! The B-32 was an effective design but ended up serving as a 'back-up' to the Boeing B-29 Superfortress. (Consolidated)

(with a wingspan of 135ft (41.15m), length of 83ft 1in (25.32m), height of 33ft (10.05m) and wing area of 1,422sq ft), the B-32 had two enormous bomb bays which could carry an internal load of 20,000lb (9,072kg) of bombs.

## B-29 Back-up

The USAAF was distressed by early teething problems with the B-29 Superfortress (last chapter) and for a time consideration was given to mass-producing the B-32 instead. As it became increasingly evident that the B-29 was going to succeed, the B-32 assumed a secondary role and was essentially a 'back-up' to the other design. Nor did the B-32 itself escape some development problems, which delayed delivery of the Dominator to XX Bomber Command in the Pacific until December 1944, some nine months after the first Superfortress.

No fewer than 115 B-32 Dominators were built and about two dozen of them reached the 386th Bomb Squadron at Okinawa before hostilities ended in the Pacific. The B-32 did, however, fly a number of combat missions and one of these aircraft may have shot down a Japanese fighter. But in the overall scheme of things, the B-32 had about as much influence as did the Russian entry into the Pacific war a week before it ended.

Also in the 'lesser known' category were the XB-33 and B-33A, both of them variations on a 'Super Marauder' which was supposed to come from the Glenn L. Martin Company. As noted earlier, the Marauder proved eminently successful during the war but the B-33 versions were not built.

## Lockheed Ventura

The Ventura – one of several low-wing, twin-engined twin-tail aircraft in the Lodestar, Hudson, Ventura and Harpoon series produced by Lockheed and its affiliate Vega – is better remembered as a general-purpose 'hack' than as a fearsome bomber, but nevertheless was operated widely by the US Navy and foreign air forces. Nearly 400 Venturas were delivered to the RAF, for whom the type was originally designed, and others to the Commonwealth Air Forces.

Many bombers turned over to the US Navy for patrol work became 'PBs' (patrol bombers), such as the already-mentioned PBJ Mitchell and PB4Y Liberator. The rather less formidable Ventura simply became a 'P' (patrol) aeroplane. Navy versions of the graceful but not very powerful Ventura included the PV-1 (over 1,600 built) used largely for anti-submarine patrol, the PV-1P reconnaissance machine with oblique cameras, and the PV-2

The Lockheed Ventura did not, perhaps, strike fear into the hearts of the Axis but it served effectively on anti-submarine patrol, in the training mission, and as an all-purpose 'hack'. Lockheed-Vega B-34 Ventura 41-38165, coded 'M-125', flies over Randolph Field in San Antonio, Texas – an important training centre – early in the war. (USAF)

Lockheed B-34 Ventura 'Doolittle'll Domore', festooned with what seems an unusual number of antennas and aerials, sitting on the ground in US Army camouflage on 17 October 1942.

Lost history? A photo acquired by the author with no details, perhaps the only surviving image of twenty-eight men and two Lockheed Venturas, veterans of a great and noble fight. Aircraft c/n. 4425 (right) was a Ventura II (AJ288) diverted from Britain and placed into US service without the B-34 designation. (via Vincent J. DiMattina, Jr)

US Navy Lockheed PV-1 Ventura patrol bombers of bomb squadron VB-135 being 'gassed up' at the airstrip in Attu, Aleutians, on 5 May 1944. The Aleutians were the only US territory invaded by Japanese troops during the war, and they later served as a base for trans-Pacific operations by PV-1s against the Japanese installation at Paramushiro in the Kuriles. The ground is thawed in this view, but it was a cold war! (via R. J. Mills Jr)

Harpoon, another anti-shipping aircraft. Some late-model PV-1s had fairly advanced search radar and added gun packs, and a handful of PV-1s were used by the Marine Corps as night fighters with the crew reduced from five to three.

The USAAF designation B-34 applies to some 200 Venturas ordered with 2,000hp Pratt & Whitney R-2800-31 engines. B-34A, B-34B and B-37 versions of the Ventura also existed. Under an agreement which gave coastal anti-shipping and anti-submarine work exclusively to the Navy, the USAAF actually halted its intended purchase of B-34s to permit the Navy to acquire PV-1s and PV-2s from the same production line. The designations RB-34, RB-34A and RB-34B were used during the war to indicate that performance operations of the Ventura in the USAAF were 'restricted', and none of the aircraft is thought to have been employed in combat.

The two USAAF designations which come next actually apply to post-war aircraft, the Northrop XB-35 flying wing and Convair B-36 strategic bomber, both outside the scope of this work. The B-37 Ventura has already been mentioned.

The little-known XB-38 represented one of several attempts during the war to take a familiar, proven bomber equipped with air-cooled radial engines and experiment with it with liquid-cooled in-line power-plants. Yes, it was the familiar B-17 Flying Fortress, in fact a B-17E converted by Vega, with unfamiliar engines. For this re-engining evaluation, power was provided by four 1,425hp Allison V-1710-89 liquid-cooled engines, the same powerplants that had been used in the early versions of the P-51 Mustang and in the Bell P-63 Kingcobra. One suspects that some politicking by the Allison Division of General Motors may have figured in this somewhat pointless exercise. In any event, the historical significance of the XB-38 was nil.

A similar experiment was conducted with a YB-29 Superfortress which was converted to take Allison V-3420 liquid-cooled engines.

## Enter the XB-39

This time the results were more impressive. In late February 1943 the programme was launched to test the Superfortress, now redesignated XB-39, with the Allison engines. The modification was done by Fisher Body Division at Cleveland and included the designing and building of new nacelles to fit on the standard firewall, as well as the actual engine installation.

Later it was decided to delay the XB-39 programme until the engines and nacelles had been tested on the Douglas B-19, modified with these powerplants to become the B-19A. Then, after many other delays, work was intensified on the XB-39 and nacelles identical to those of the XB-19A were used. The first flight was made on 9 December 1944 and

US Navy Lockheed PV-2 Harpoon in flight. (USN)

Two views of a static test-bed used by Lockheed to run up the Allison liquid-cooled engines mounted on the XB-38 (41-2401), an aircraft which, apart from the engines, was identical to the B-17 Fortress. Liquid-cooled engines were also tested on the XB-39, which was otherwise identical to the B-29 Superfortress. In neither instance did the Allison powerplants prove superior to radial engines already in use. (Lockheed)

A Boeing design, a Lockheed conversion, with Allison engines: the XB-38 Fortress bomber on 4 October 1943. Note airscoop between engines on each wing. (Lockheed)

flight-testing was taken over by the Air Technical Services Command at Wright Field, Ohio.

The sole XB-39, 41-36954 'Spirit of Lincoln,' was fitted at Cleveland with four V-3420-A16 engines developing 2,600hp at sea-level. Later, at the Allison Installation Engineering Section at Plant 10 in Cleveland, V-3420-A18 engines were installed. These were improved structurally over the -A16s but had the same power output.

History continued without a ripple. As an official history states, 'Although the XB-39 was not placed in production, a great deal was learned on the advantages of liquid-cooled engines for multi-engine aircraft.'

The final USAAF designations for wartime bombers were YB-40 and XB-41, both of these being flying gun batteries made from, respectively, the B-17 Fortress and B-24 Liberator. In the case of the YB-40, it is not clear how the aircraft acquired such a late designation when, in fact, it preceded bombers having lower numbers.

Lockheed, or more correctly the firm's Vega affiliate, converted Boeing B-17F 41-24341 as an escort aircraft with the designation XB-40, later YB-40. The aircraft was first flown on 10 November 1942.

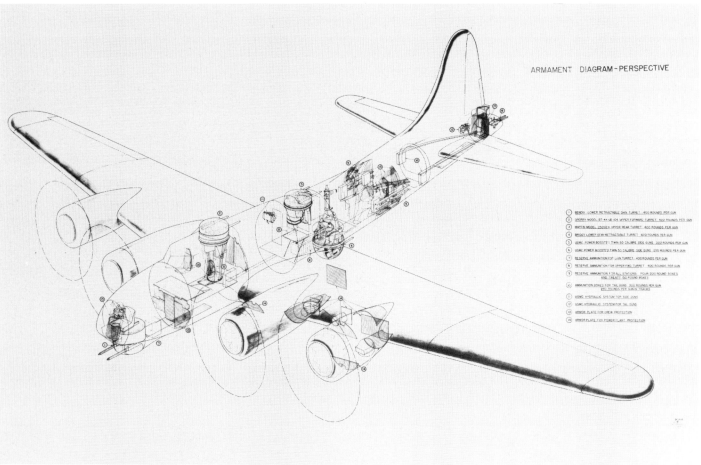

ARMAMENT DIAGRAM - PERSPECTIVE

**Above:** Another application of liquid-cooled engines to a bomber normally powered by air-cooled radials: the XB-39 was a Boeing B-29 Superfortress (41-36954, 'Spirit of Lincoln') modified with four Allison V-3420-As. The XB-38 apparently had nothing wrong with it but did not offer a significant improvement and was not ordered into production. (USAF)

**Left and right:** The Lockheed YB-40 was a B-17 Fortress converted under the direction of the USAAF Air Technical Services Command (ATSC) into a 'flying gunship' designed to protect other Fortresses from enemy fighters. One source indicates these aircraft were known at the time as 'Flying Hedgehogs'. The cutaway drawing shows the armament diagram of the YB-40, while the close-up photo shows guns intended to be brought to bear on Messerschmitts and Focke-Wulfs. (Lockheed)

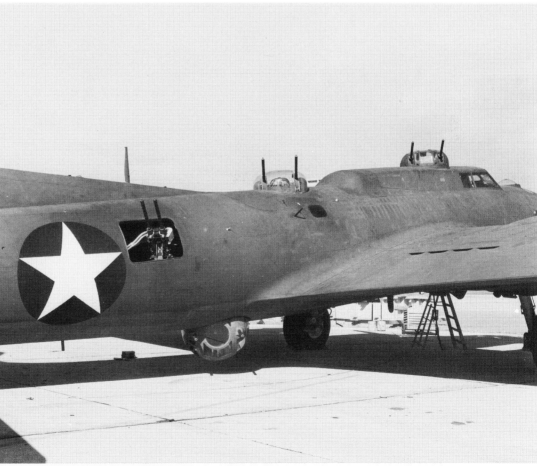

The idea was to create a heavily armed and armoured bomber derivative capable of vastly increasing the output of machine-gun fire from a bomber formation, thus increasing the formation's protection against enemy fighters. The XB-40 carried standard Fortress armament plus twin 0.50in (12.7mm) guns in a chin turret, in a second dorsal turret (substituting for the Fortress's hand-held weapon amidships) and in each waist position (again, replacing hand-held guns). The XB-40 Fortress carried no bombs but embarked on a mission carrying 11,135 rounds of machine-gun ammunition!

The conversion of twenty Vega-built B-17Fs to YB-40 service-test standard and four more as TB-40 trainers was transferred to Douglas's Tulsa, Oklahoma, plant.

Unlike most of the bombers covered in this section on lesser-known types, a few YB-40s actually reached the combat zone, operating with the 92nd Bomb Group at Alconbury, England. The aircraft were found to have sluggish and difficult flying characteristics in combat and after a few missions in May and June 1943 were retired. The chin turret, however, was eventually adopted by the definitive B-17G Fortress.

## Consolidated XB-41

Less successful, however much it was modelled on the same idea, was the Consolidated XB-41, a conversion of a B-24D for the same escort mission. Whereas thirteen YB-40 Fortresses were built, only a single XB-41 appeared.

This variation on the ubiquitous Liberator was not a success. Furthermore, in time it was discovered that the USAAF already had the escort fighter it needed – the North American P-51 Mustang. When Mustangs began escorting Fortresses over Berlin, interest in a heavy four-engined 'flying gunship' virtually disappeared.

It should not be thought that the US Navy had no role in the development of bomber aviation during the war. If the SBD Dauntless and TBF Avenger were 'bombers' – albeit for different bombing roles – so too were a host of other designs which never went beyond the drawing-boards or reached operational service. If the Consolidated PBY Catalina and Martin PBM Mariner were 'bombers' – here the consensus is decidedly less clear – what about lesser-known types such as the Consolidated PB2Y Coronado? The latter, a four-engined long-range flying-boat developed in the pre-war years, never carried or dropped a bomb in anger, nor did the Martin PB2M-1 Mars which was correctly redesignated JRM-1 to reflect its role as a general-purpose transport. Both, however, provided the Navy with extensive knowledge on the operation of large, multi-engined aircraft which proved important in the post-war years when the admirals wanted their own strategic bomber force.

In fact, the war produced a number of changes in US Navy design philosophy. An important change was the deletion of the scout role from aircraft designed for dive-bombing, making it possible for a 'Dauntless replacement' to be flown by only one man. Douglas produced no fewer than three aircraft which did not make the grade as a latter-generation Dauntless – the BTD-1, BT2D-1 and TB2D-1 were all eminently forgettable – but when it proved essential to create such a design, Ed Heinemann's design team did not fail. Given less than 24 hours to produce an effective design and cooped up in the Shoreham Hotel in Washington, DC, Heinemann and his colleagues sketched out the BT2D-1 Dauntless II, an aeroplane which took to the air before the Axis surrender. Not truly a part of the World War II story, this single-seater indeed replaced the Dauntless and was soon redesignated AD-1 Skyraider. It went on to fight in Korea and Vietnam.

The US Navy's long-range patrol aircraft are generally covered in the sections of this volume which deal with their USAAF equivalents. The PBJ Mitchell and PB4Y Liberator are examples. A number of more successful Navy bombers are covered in the following chapter. To be certain, the word 'bomber' makes one think first of Flying Fortress or Liberator and only much later of the aeroplanes in sea blue which carried out the Navy's mission.

## Design Successes

From XB-15 to XB-41 (with the odd Navy type thrown in) the lesser-known US bombers of World War II represented successes, setbacks and innovation – the inspiration of a few able officers and the offspring of an industry which seemed to have unlimited potential and which produced the greatest aerial armada the world has ever seen.

When the United States entered the war in December 1941 it was still being argued whether large bombers should have four engines. By the end – after B-29 Superfortresses sought by Air Corps generals and produced by American industry laid Japan's home islands to waste – the USAAF was developing jet bombers and flying wings. In remarkably few years, the Americans went from aircraft which could carry a few 500lb (227kg) bombs to the capability to carry an atomic weapon that recreated the fires of hell.

In half a decade, bomber aviation had advanced more than in all the previous forty years.

# Navy Bombers

The outward appearance of the Consolidated Catalina changed little over the years as more advanced versions were developed. Aircraft 'six' of Patrol Squadron Six (VP-6) is the first production PBY-1 (originally P3Y-1), bureau number 0102, and is seen beached on 1 March 1939. Early Catalinas like this one were flying-boats only; amphibious versions came later in the war. (USN via R. J. Mills, Jr)

**V**ital to the American war effort during the critical years 1941–45 was the procession of naval bombing aeroplanes which poured out from the seemingly inexhaustible resources of American industry. Like the scout and dive-bombers already discussed, patrol bomber (PB) and torpedo-bomber (TB) designs progressed through the war years, beginning with some of the oldest aircraft types to see battle (Catalina, Devastator) and concluding with some of the best (Mariner, Avenger).

Torpedo-bombers, in fact, were not used all that often by the Americans (unlike the British) to drop torpedoes, partly because of problems with the torpedoes and because, as one officer puts it, 'that mission was just too damned dangerous'. They were used to drop bombs in support of Marines island-hopping across the Pacific.

Nor were patrol bombers always used for the classic patrol mission, the 'surface vessel fleet-shadowing activity', as one man puts it. Most patrol aircraft had their responsibilities split between anti-surface warfare and level bombing. The best of the patrol bombers, the PBY Catalina, was a jack of all trades. 'It would be easier to find a mission the PBY didn't perform than to name all those it did.'

## Enter the Catalina

The Consolidated PBY Catalina was the US Navy's prime wartime workhorse for long-range ocean patrols, flying those gruelling and thankless missions which subjected the crew to weary hours of boredom broken by an occasional chance to drop a bomb or fire a gun.

The Catalina was far from graceful – one pilot called it 'the ugliest aircraft the Navy has ever had' – but even though its replacement (the PBM Mariner) had been ordered before the US entry into the war, the Catalina was the predominant patrol plane throughout the conflict. 3,272 examples of all variants were built, among them 1,854 flying-boats and 1,418 amphibians, with no fewer than seven manufacturing plants turning out 'Cats'.

The Catalina was far from speedy – there were jokes about the danger of bird strikes from behind, or about needing a calendar rather than a stopwatch in order to rendezvous with a convoy – but if its speed of 175mph (282km/h) on a good day was no record-setter, the PBY managed to get there and get the job done. One destroyed a submarine. Another earned a Medal of Honor for its pilot.

Designed by Isaac M. (Mac) Laddon, a gifted seaplane engineer and director of Consolidated Aircraft, the first Catalina was designated XP3Y-1 (bureau number 9459) and was first flown from Lake Erie on 28 March 1935. The Consolidated contract for sixty PBY-1 flying-boats at $90,000 each was signed on 29 June 1935, with deliveries of the first aeroplanes commencing in September 1936.

After the flight of the prototype near Buffalo, production was transferred to San Diego and the first production Catalina joined the Navy on 5 October 1936 when it was taxied from the Consolidated plant in Lindbergh Field across the airfield to Patrol Squadron 11F (VP-11F).

Although the external appearance of this 'ugly duckling' changed little over the war years, advanced versions kept introducing new items of equipment and new capabilities, including the amphibious capability which came with the XPBY-5A variant in December 1939.

Among the manufacturers of the Catalina were: Consolidated Aircraft Corporation at Buffalo, New York (XP3Y-1); Consolidated Aircraft Corporation, San Diego, California (PBY-1, PBY-2, PBY-3, PBY-4, PBY-5); Consolidated Aircraft Corporation, New Orleans, Louisiana (PBY-5, PBY-5A, PBY-6A); Naval Aircraft Factory, Philadelphia, Pennsylvania (PBN-2); Boeing of Canada, Vancouver, British Columbia (PB2B-1, PB2B-2); and Canadian Vickers Ltd, Montreal, Quebec (PBV-1A, OA-10A).

'Dumbo', Catalina, the 'Black Cat', whatever they called it – Canso was an official RCAF name – the old, slow, yet incredibly dependable aircraft was

Apparently one of the 'Black Cats' used for exceedingly dangerous rescue missions later in the war, this Catalina sports Yagi antennas under both wings and a much-faded paint scheme. The aircraft is a PBY-5 with an unknown bureau number ending in 465, belonging to Patrol Squadron Five Two (VP-52) and seen in flight on 10 February 1944. (USN via R. J. Mills, Jr)

widely modified in the field, so that each PBY ended up being a little different from all others. Enterprising mechanics who laboured under difficult conditions to keep them flying often found the PBY design highly adaptable, to the extent of installing different engines on several instances.

The principal versions of the Catalina included:

**PBY-1,** the first production aircraft, powered by 900hp Pratt & Whitney R-1830-64 engines, 60 of which were manufactured in San Diego in 1936–37.

**PBY-2,** with various internal modifications, 50 manufactured in San Deigo, 1937–38.

**PBY-3,** powered by 1,000hp R-1830-66 engines with other internal changes, 66 manufactured in San Diego, 1937–38.

**PBY-4,** powered by 1,050hp R-1830-72 engines, 32 built in San Diego, 1938–39.

**PBY-5,** powered by 1,200hp R-1830-92 engines, 586 built in San Diego, 1942–43, including British Catalina I through IV models.

**PBY-5A,** first amphibious version with retractable tricycle landing gear, 803 built by various manufacturers, deliveries to Britain, Free French Forces, Soviet Union.

**PBN-1,** given the nickname 'Nomad', although everybody called it Catalina, this version was built by the Naval Aircraft Factory, Philadelphia, with extensive hull, wing and tail changes; 156 built including 137 delivered to Soviet Union.

**PBY-6A,** amphibious version of PBN-1 (USAAF OA-10B), 175 built in New Orleans in 1945, including
some delivered to Soviet Union.

**PB2B-1,** Boeing-built PBY-5, 240 delivered in 1943–44 including some for Australia and New Zealand.

**PB2B-2,** Boeing-built PBY-6A, 67 built in 1944–45 including some to Britain and Australia.

A typical Catalina (to use the PBY-5A amphibian as our example) was credited, as has been noted, with a maximum speed of 175mph (282km/h). Cruising speed on patrol was 113mph (182km/h). Initial climb rate was 620ft (189m) per minute, service ceiling 13,000ft (3,960m) and range 2,350 miles (3,782km).

While armament varied, the typical Catalina was armed with a 0.50in (12.7mm) machine-gun in each waist blister, two more such guns in the bow turret located on the tip of the nose ahead of the pilot, and a 0.30in (7.62mm) in the rear ventral hatch. External wing racks enabled the craft to carry four bombs of up to 1,000lb (454kg) each.

## Heroic Actions

There were any number of actions involving the famous flying-boat/amphibian. To cite but one heroic action in the 'Cat':

Aircraft 'five' of VP-1 is a Consolidated PBY-3 Catalina, apparently flying over San Diego. The patrol bombers in this series were produced under Navy contract number 51701 with the first machine being delivered to a squadron on 30 July 1937. Pre-war natural metal gave way to blue exterior when the fighting began. (USN via Lt-Cdr Dave Parsons)

'Accident – mud flats – Ooops!' reads the original caption to this Catalina photograph. What appears to be a Boeing PB2B-1 variant of the famous Consolidated design (note distinctive high tail), it is wearing post-war national insignia and is sitting high and dry, perhaps because the tide went out. (USN via Dave Parsons)

All-black Catalina, as seen from a wingman, prowls off the coast of New Guinea in about 1944. (USN)

Numerous Catalinas survived the war to be used in various roles. To celebrate the 75th anniversary of US naval aviation, two were painted in a rough approximation of pre-World War II markings and flown across the Atlantic on a commemorative flight, one of the pilots being Rear Admiral Ron Marryott, Deputy Director of the Defense Intelligence Agency. One of these commemorative Catalinas is shown during a visit to Andrews AFB, Maryland, on 5 May 1986. (Howard Wheeler)

On 15 February 1944 Lt Jg Nathan G. Gordon was flying a PBY-5 Catalina configured as a 'Black Cat' rescue craft in support of a Fifth Air Force B-25 Mitchell attack against Kavieng Harbour on New Ireland. Gordon spotted an empty liferaft, touched down on the water, but found the raft empty. After take-off Gordon's crew sighted survivors of a Mitchell crew in the water near the abandoned raft. Gordon landed again and shut down both engines to rescue the men bobbing about in the water.

Gordon's Catalina came under heavy fire from Japanese shore batteries. Bursting shells kicked up geysers of water around him. Under fire, he completed the rescue and took off – only to have his Catalina crew discover yet another group of Mitchell survivors down in the sea. Gordon landed again, shut down an engine, and picked up three suvivors. He took off again only to be called back to rescue yet another Mitchell crew! This crew was struggling to paddle a liferaft out to sea from 600 yards offshore and was coming under fire from the Japanese shore guns.

Gordon took himself perilously close to the enemy, bringing his aircraft under fire. While shells exploded around him, Gordon struggled aloft once more, now carrying no fewer than fifteen USAAF rescuees. Gordon received the Medal of Honor, the highest American award, for this action at the controls of PBY-5 Catalina bureau number 08434, side number '71', 'The Arkansas Traveler'. But the real point of his story is that it illustrates the enormous ability of the Catalina to survive under pressure and to carry enormous loads beyond any ever foreseen.

US Navy patrol squadrons which operated the famous Catalina included VP-6, VP-7, VP-9, VP-11, VP-13, VP-21, VP-34, VP-52, VP-54, VP-81, VP-101 and VO-102. Post-war Catalinas were operated by the US Coast Guard and many found their way on to the US civil register where perhaps as many as eighty are still listed today. The lesser-known USAAF OA-10A and OA-10B versions served well into the 1950s.

## Followed by the Coronado

No sooner had Consolidated designers created the Catalina than the manufacturer progressed to the much bigger Consolidated Model 29, alias PB2Y-1 Coronado – an imposing, four-engined patrol bomber flying-boat which first flew on 17 December 1937.

A huge aircraft which would have been formidable as a bomber, the Coronado existed in PB2Y-1 through PB2Y-5 versions and began service with the US Navy's patrol squadron VP-13 in 1940. Its role as

Big, cavernous, impressive, this Consolidated PB2Y-2 Coronado, seen slicing through the air on 3 July 1942, was at one time a candidate for the job of launching the first American bombing mission on Japan, a task given instead to carrier-based B-25 Mitchells. The Coronado could have been a formidable patrol bomber, but was used mostly for transport duties. (USN via R. J. Mills, Jr)

a patrol bomber was limited, but VP-13 was still flying the Coronado on its original warlike mission during the invasion of Okinawa when seaplanes played a vital role. Most Coronados spent most of the war as transports, one of the more than 210 built serving as the personal 'barge' for Admiral Chester Nimitz. Others were briefly the backbone of Pacific operations for the Naval Air Transport Service.

Powered by four 1,200hp Pratt & Whitney R-1830-88 Twin Wasp radial engines, the PB2Y Coronado weighted 40,935lb (18,568kg) empty, rather less than its formidable size would suggest, and 68,000lb (30,844kg) fully loaded. Dimensions included wingspan 115ft (35.05m), length 79ft 3in (24.16m), height 27ft 6in (8.38m), and wing area 1,780sq ft.

The Coronado cruised at 141mph (227km/h) and had a maximum speed of 223mph (359km/h), making it rather faster than its Catalina stablemate.

The Consolidated Model 31, or XP4Y-1, was a large twin-engined patrol bomber similar in appearance to the Coronado and unofficially named the Corregidor. The aircraft performed well but difficulties in the development of its 2,300hp R-3350-8 Cyclone engines caused an order for 200 to be cancelled, with only the prototype actually flown. The R-3350 engine, of course, was sorely needed for the B-29 and many other aircraft types designed around this powerplant suffered when B-29 production was assigned top priority.

## Martin Mariner

The Catalina was already long in the tooth when the United States entered hostilities. Its intended re-placement was the Martin PBM Mariner. Newer, bigger, prettier (though not by much), more sea-worthy and far roomier on the inside, the Mariner never did replace the 'Cat,' but it served equally as valiantly and became as much loved and appreciated by crews.

Rather different in philosophy from the Catalina, with a deeper and more cavernous fuselage and gull wings, the PBM or Martin Model 162 resulted from development work which began in 1937. The aircraft flew for the first time on 18 February 1939.

An unusual and interesting aspect of the development of this aircraft is that the Glenn L. Martin company built a scaled-down 'proof of concept' seaplane, the Model 162-A, prototype prior to the actual Mariner. The Model 162-A was powered by a single Glenn L. Martin Chevrolet inverted four-cylinder 120hp engine which was linked to both 7ft-diameter propellers via V-belts and was flown by a single pilot. In fact, the success of the Model 162-A made it possible to speed up the production of Mariners. This intriguing test aeroplane has survived and belongs to the Smithsonian Institution's National Air and Space Museum.

The US Navy formally accepted the prototype Mariner (bureau number 0796) on 7 September 1939 and delivery of production PBM-1s began a year later to squadrons VP-55 and VP-56.

The Mariner was produced in the following versions, which served not only as patrol bombers but also as anti-submarine craft, transports and utility aeroplanes:

**PBM-1** was the initial production version with a full fit of armament unlike the prototypes. Compared

The Martin Model 162-A was a ⅜-scale model of the PBM-1 Mariner, seen on its cradle. First seen publicly in 1937, the Model 162-A was a cost-efficient way to test the Mariner design and may have saved time and money when the PBM-1 itself flew. (Martin via Lt-Cdr Dave Parsons)

Aircraft '9' of Patrol Squadron 55 (VP-55) was one of the first Martin Mariners and was delivered to the US Navy on 4 November 1938. The aircraft had retractable floats. The paint scheme on Mariners changed significantly after the outbreak of war, but the appearance of the aircraft remained about the same. (USN)

A Consolidated PB2Y-6 Coronado beached, possibly at San Diego, on 8 February 1945. (USN via Lt-Cdr Dave Parsons)

Wearing the light-coloured camouflage used for anti-submarine operations in tropical climes, three PBM-3S Mariners pass the imposing 130ft statue of Christ the Redeemer on 2,310ft Corcovado Peak, approaching Brazil's Rio de Janeiro. The first aeroplane in the PBM-3S series was delivered on 30 August 1943. (USN)

Most Martin PBM Mariners were not amphibians and had to be brought ashore by laborious beaching procedures, to be wheeled around on land on multiple dollies. Post-war action at Naval Air Station Jacksonville, Florida, on 21 September 1955 shows PBM-5 Mariner 84729 (EC-8) of patrol squadron VP-34. (USN)

with the prototypes, the 'dash one' had a redesigned and improved bow turret. Twenty were delivered.

**XPBM-2** was a one-off model (bureau number 1247) with increased fuel capacity, reinforced structure, and attachments which permitted it to be launched by catapult. In 1942 the XPBM-2 was successfully catapulted from a small vessel known as a Catapult Lighter. The intention was to use a surface vessel to support the aircraft and get it closer to its objective.

**PBM-3** Mariners were all purpose-built with letter suffixes indicating specialized missions, including the PBM-3S anti-submarine, PBM-3R transport, PBM-3E equipped with search radar and other electronics, PBM-3Cs for anti-submarine work, PBM-3Ds for long-range Pacific missions and the PBM-3B which was the American designation for the British Mariner Mark II.

**PBM-4E** was a more powerful Mariner with increased electronics gear and other items of equipment.

**PBM-5** was the final major production version and was the first aircraft in the series to be equipped for JATO (jet-assisted take-off) bottles, which were used on combat missions for the first time during combat at Iwo Jima in February 1945. Sub-variants included the PBM-5A amphibian, PBM-5E with electronics gear, PBM-5C used in missile tests, and PBM-5N night and all-weather aircraft. Only one

example of the last-named appeared, bureau number 98606.

**PBM-6** was the US Navy's nomenclature for a single PBM-3D (bureau number 45274) which was modified to a new configuration. No information about this aircraft has ever been revealed.

A typical Mariner was powered by two 1,900hp Wright R-2600-22 Cyclone radial engines, had a maximum speed of 211mph (340km/h), and was armed with eight 0.50in (12.7mm) machine-guns with a bomb load of 8,000lb (3,628kg). The aircraft weighed 33,175lb (15,048kg) empty and 58,000lb (26,308kg) loaded.

Patrol squadrons flying the Mariner during wartime operations included VP-16, VP-21, VP-32, VP-74, VP-202, VP-206, VP-208, VP-211, VP-214, as well as 'patrol bomber' squadrons (a redesignation of the function) VPB-13, VPB-17, VPB-18, VPB-19, VPB-21, VPB-26, VPB-216, and transport squadrons VR-6 and VR-8.

Thirty-one Mariners were delivered to Britain, of which twelve were passed on to Australia. In postwar years, a number of these aircraft served as search and rescue and anti-submarine aircraft with allied navies, the Dutch Navy being an example.

The only surviving Mariner in the US is PBM-5A bureau number 122071, which belongs to the Smithsonian Institution but is on loan to the Pima County Air Museum.

Looking far more futuristic than the flying-boats it was intended to replace, the Boeing PBB-1 Sea Ranger was a formidable aircraft and would have been highly effective had the war against Japan continued longer. As it turned out, the success of earlier aircraft made it unnecessary to put the PBB-1 into production. (USN via Lt-Cdr Dave Parsons)

## Martin Mars

The Mariner was of course a modest aircraft compared with Martin's giant, four-engined XPB2M-1 Mars patrol bomber which was ordered on 23 August 1938 and first flew on 3 July 1942 with Ken Ebel as pilot. It was powered by four 2,200hp Curtiss Wright R-3350-8 engines and at the time was considered the world's largest aircraft. The Martin Mars weighed 160,000lb.

The Navy quickly decided that the Mars should be a transport. The prototype was therefore redesignated PB2M-1R and operated by transport squadron VR-8 at NAS Patuxent River, Maryland. This impressive machine was transferred to VR-2 at NAS Alameda, California, in 1944. Five subsequent aircraft in the series were built from the ground up as JRM-1 transports and one more as a JRM-2 transport (bureau numbers 76819/76824). The sole JRM-2, the 'Caroline Mars' (bureau number 76824), differed in having four 3,000hp Pratt & Whitney R-4360-4 (later R-4360) engines in longer nacelles.

As a footnote, when the Doolittle raid on Tokyo was being planned, an alternative idea was to use very large flying-boats and have them create their own refuelling locations by leapfrogging across the Pacific before bombing Japan. The idea of using carrier-based B-25 Mitchells clearly had greater merit and was adopted instead.

## Torpedo-Bombers

Our examination of US bombers of World War II has now included a *tour d'horizon* of the Navy's scout bomber and patrol bomber aeroplanes. Not as glamorous or as well known as Fortress or Mitchell, these were bombers nonetheless. Likewise, the US Navy's torpedo-bomber force was a vital part of the aerial armada which won the war. Even though the President of the United States flew one, torpedo-bombers rarely get much credit or attention in the USA. They deserve more.

The torpedo-bomber story begins with an aircraft even older and slower than the Catalina, namely the Douglas TBD Devastator which flew in prototype form on 15 April 1935.

A straightforward and conventional aeroplane, mostly of metal construction but with some fabric surfaces, the Devastator impressed Navy officials

The largest aircraft to serve in the US Navy, the Martin Mars began life as the PB2M-1 patrol bomber, but before it could ever drop a bomb in anger, the Navy decided to employ the type as a transport and ordered the JRM-1 Mars version, seen in this post-war formation. (Martin)

enough for them to place an order for 129 TBD-1 aircraft on 3 February 1936. This 'taildragger' carrier-based torpedo-bomber was initially powered by an 800hp Pratt & Whitney XR-1830-60 radial engine (R-1830-64 in production versions) and had a crew of three comprising pilot, bombardier/navigator and radioman/gunner.

The initial batch of production TBD-1 Devastators was delivered to squadron VT-3 in 1937. Almost half a decade later when the US fleet clashed with the Japanese in the Coral Sea and at Midway, the heavy and rather sluggish Devastator was still in service with torpedo-bomber squadrons aboard the few carriers available to the US in the early stages of the conflict.

One of the early sagas of the war was the story of Torpedo Squadron Eight (VT-8), under Lt Cdr John Waldron, which took its slow and vulnerable Devastators into withering enemy fire to attack Japanese warships in a futile effort. VT-8 lost every aircraft and every man in its 'Charge of the Light Brigade' attack on Japanese ships; the sole exception was Ensign George Gay who was dragged out of the ocean by an intrepid PBY Catalina crew and survived to receive the Medal of Honor. A fate almost as bad befell the small detachment of the same squadron operating the newer TBF Avenger, of which more later.

The TBD-1 Devastator had a maximum speed of 206mph (332km/h) and a service ceiling of 18,100ft (6,039m). The aircraft weighed 6,182lb (2,804kg) empty and 10,194lb (4,624kg) fully loaded. Midway through the war, Devastators were withdrawn from front-line service after what added up to a very brief operational career.

A number of one-off Douglas designs included the XTB2D-1 Skypirate, an unsuccessful candidate for further US Navy production orders. While the Douglas firm was no slouch at creating warplanes, especially for naval operations, it was the legendary Grumann 'Iron Works' which designed, developed, and received authority to produce the Devastator replacement or next-generation torpedo-bomber.

## Enter the Avenger

In 1940 the Navy ordered two XTBF-1 prototypes from Grumman to compete with the less successful Vought XTBU-1, which later became the Consolidated TBY-1 Sea Wolf. Bill Schwendler and the Grumman design team produced a bulky and formidable aircraft of all-metal construction, except for its fabric control surfaces, which was capable of a maximum speed of 267mph (430km/h). The hefty and rather portly Avenger flew for the first time with Bob Hall at the controls (bureau number 2539) on 1 August 1941 and, like most Grumman products during this period, it was relatively free of development difficulties. Grumman's products had such an extraordinary record of working right the first time that no manufacturer has matched it before or since.

Through no fault of the design, the Avenger programme suffered a setback on 28 November 1941 when an in-flight fire in the bomb bay forced test pilot Hobart Cook and crewmate Gordon Israel to bail out. The second prototype (bureau number 2540) flew on 15 December 1941, and it was the proximity to the time of Pearl Harbor that led to the name Avenger.

The TBF-1 was then the biggest and heaviest aircraft ever designed from the outset for carrier operations. It was powered by a 1,700hp Wright R-2600 Cyclone double-row radial. This was a big engine, but not nearly as big as the TBF-1's rather

**Above: Formation of six Douglas TBD-1 Devastator dive-bombers in peaceful skies in 1939, the crews almost certainly unaware of the horror that awaited them and their aircraft at Midway. The sturdy but aged TBD-1 was perhaps the oldest American bomber of the war and was no match for the frenzied wall of anti-aircraft fire that could be put up by the Japanese fleet. (USN via R. J. Mills, Jr)**

**Top right: Aboard the carrier the Japanese didn't sink at Pearl Harbor, the USS *Enterprise* (CV-6). This flight deck scene in April 1942 shows Douglas TBD-1 Devastators with rough seas in the background. When Torpedo Squadron Eight under Cdr John Waldron used these ageing bombers to attack the Japanese fleet at Midway, every single Devastator was shot out of the sky and only one member of the squadron, Ensign George Gay, survived. (Robert F. Dorr)**

**Right: The Douglas TBD-1 Devastator took some very brave men into battle – very slowly. In this pre-war view, TBD-1 bureau number 0318, in the foreground, is among several Torpedo Squadron Six (VT-6) Devastators heading out on a mission. (USN)**

large fuselage which caused some to call it 'The
Pregnant Beast'. Another nickname was 'Turkey',
which in World War II had no negative connotation
and simply referred to size. The Avenger was big all
right, but scarcely unconventional – another 'taildragger' with folding outer wing panels for carrier
stowage. Under the wing was a large internal bay
with hydraulically operated folding doors for a
torpedo, mine, or bombs of up to 2,000lb (907kg).

Perched high on the top was the pilot, equipped
with a 0.30in (7.62mm) gun firing ahead. Aft of the
wing in a rear compartment was the bombardier/
gunner, and above him was the rear gunner. Unlike
Dauntless and Devastator gunners who hung out in
their shirtsleeves in an open cockpit, the Avenger's
upper rear gun operator sat inside a power-driven
enclosed rotary turret.

Because the turret was such a distinctive feature
on the Avenger, it may be worth a few more words.
Grumman engineer Oscar Olsen is credited with
finding a solution to the Navy's specification for a
power turret, despite the difficulties of weight and
traverse inherent in mechanical and hydraulic
turrets. Olsen's is believed to be the first electrically
operated turret to be used successfully.

The Avenger cruised at 150mph (240km/h; and
had a service ceiling of 23,400ft (7,130m) and range
of 1,130 miles (1,819km). The relatively long range
of this aircraft was to prove important in carrier
operations in the Pacific where fuel and endurance
limits almost prevented success in more than one
battle.

This big torpedo-bomber had wing span of 54ft
2in (16.51m), length of 40ft (12.19m), height of 16ft
5in (5.00m) and wing area of 490sq ft (45.52m$^2$).
Principal variants of the Avenger were:

**TBF-1** (TBM-1) was the initial production version
and had sub-variants which included the TBF-1E
with additional avionics, the TBF-1J winterized for
all-weather operations, the TBF-1L with a retractable
searchlight in the bomb bay and the TBF-1CP and
TBF-1P photo-reconnaissance versions.

**TBF-1B** was the US Navy designation for the
Royal Navy's Tarpon I, as the aircraft was initially
called in British service (although the name Avenger
was more widely used and became official in January
1944). 402 were delivered.

**TBM-1C** was the British Tarpon II, 334 of which
were delivered.

**XTBF-2** was a one-off variant powered by the
1,900hp Wright XR-2600-10 engine. It is not clear
how this version differed from other models with
other versions of the same engines.

**TBF-3** (TBM-3) was the version with increased
structural members in the wing to render the aircraft

more sturdy for shipboard operations. The XTBF-3
prototype was built without the standard power
turret and all but two in this series were built as
TBM-3s by General Motors. Included in TBM-3
production were a further 222 British machines,
designated Tarpon III.

**XTBM-4** was a General Motors-built prototype
with a strengthened fuselage. The aircraft performed
well, but by the time it appeared the war was ending
so no production order was placed.

## Avenger in Combat

The first operational TBF-1 Avengers appeared at the
Battle of Midway, the same action in which the
Dauntless turned the tide while the Devastator
suffered terrible losses. A detachment of six Avengers of Torpedo Squadron Eight (VT-8) under Lt
Langdon K. Fieberling arrived at Midway on 1 June
1942 and was scrambled against the Japanese carrier
force four days later. The Avenger fared little better
than the hapless Devastator in this crucial action.
Five of the six Avengers were shot down during the
fighting, with a sixth, piloted by Ensign Bert Earnest,
badly damaged. (Research by Tom Doll indicates
that the six Avengers at Midway were 00380, 00383,
00384, 00391, 00398 and 00399.)

Earnest nursed his badly damaged TBF-1 (bureau
number 00380) back to Midway. He had a dead
gunner and a wounded radio-operator. As confirmed
by research done by Barrett Tillman and Tom Doll
of the Tailhook Association, Earnest's aircraft was a
mess: he had been forced to unload his torpedo in
the midst of battle and had had his elevator cables
severed by Japanese fire. He was unable to get his
landing gear to extend fully. Earnest had no choice
but to crash-land on the beach at Midway, a
courageous act which saved the life of his wounded
radioman, RM3/C Harry Ferrier.

Bert Earnest, Harry Ferrier and George Gay were
the only survivors among forty-eight pilots and
aircrewmen who went to war at Midway in Devastators and Avengers.

Grumman built TBF-1 through TBF-3 versions
before demand for the Avenger became so great that
Eastern Division of General Motors was engaged to
build corresponding TBM-1 through TBM-3 aircraft.
There were relatively few significant changes in the
various models.

In due course, a British invention – airborne radar
– was added to the TBF Avenger. Westinghouse ASB
or ASP-4 radar went into a pod under the right wing.
395 Avengers, some of them equipped with this new
gadget, were exported to Britain's Fleet Air Arm.
Overall, no fewer than 9,939 Avengers were built.

Baptism of fire for the Avenger at Midway was far from successful but the Avenger became the Allies' principal shipboard torpedo-bomber. As for Bert Earnest, he flew TBFs and TBMs at Guadalcanal and later in Philippine operations, earning no fewer than three awards of the Navy Cross, the second highest award for valour. Earnest accumulated 1,000 hours and 255 carrier landings in the Avenger.

Another man who flew the Avenger was a young ensign named George Bush.

On 2 September 1944 Lt Jg George Bush was a pilot with Torpedo Squadron Five One (VT-51) aboard the aircraft-carrier San Jacinto (CVL-30) in the North Pacific. The one-time youngest pilot in US naval aviation set forth that morning on one of the 58 combat missions he was to complete during the war.

His target was a Japanese radio station on Chichi Jima, 600 miles (960km) south-west of Japan in the Bonin Islands. Bush and his two crewmates attacked the island through heavy anti-aircraft fire coming from gun emplacements hidden in mountains. Tiny black puffs of smoke erupted around the Avenger as Bush approached the target and went into a steep dive – so steep that he said later it felt like standing on his head. Very close to the target, Bush was hit.

He felt his plane thrown upwards from the impact of the hit. In a courageous move, Bush pressed on to the target, releasing his four 500lb (227kg) bombs and causing damaging hits with them. For pressing home the attack under difficult circumstances, Bush was later awarded the Distinguished Flying Cross.

The future American president could not get his aircraft home however. Heading out to sea, he and his crew were engulfed in flames and smoke. Bush and one of his crewmen baled out. The other, dead or seriously injured, went down with the Avenger. The other crewman also died when his parachute failed to open properly.

Bush parachuted safely into the water and was spared capture by a Japanese boat when a VT-51 wingman, Lt Doug West, flew in low with his Avenger and strafed the boat. Circling fighters transmitted Bush's plight and position to the US submarine Finback (SS-230), some 16 miles (26km) from the island. Bush was rescued by the submarine. Old motion picture of him coming aboard the vessel was used in his 1988 presidential campaign. (As a matter of interest, Bush remained aboard the submarine until the completion of its war cruise and was depth-charged several times, an experience which former Navy Secretary John Lehman describes as good preparation for the White House.)

Some reports have indicated that one of the passengers aboard Mr Bush's Avenger was in fact a family friend who at the last moment took the place of a regularly assigned crewman – and died. There can be no doubt that President Bush – who will almost certainly be the last American president to have served in World War II – was a genuine hero whose achievements as an Avenger pilot have always been underplayed.

Bush's aircraft, the Avenger, proved to be a potent adversary to Japanese fleets in the Pacific and to German U-boats in the Atlantic, and one of them even shot down a Zero fighter.

The British Avengers played an important role in supporting naval operations by US forces. A number of British Avenger pilots have been lobbying in recent years to make their contribution better known.

## Torpedo Troubles

As much as has been written about torpedo-bombers, it is frequently overlooked that the torpedo-bombing mission was risky and – in American eyes – perhaps marginal in terms of likely results. The Avenger was a solid aeroplane with an impossible job to perform. And throughout World War II difficulties with the US Navy's Mark 13 aerial torpedo continually undermined the effectiveness of the Avenger's fine aeronautical design.

The original Mark 13 torpedo was limited to drops from an altitude of under 100ft (30.48m) and under a speed of 100mph (161km/h), making it necessary for the Avenger pilot to sacrifice his aeroplane's good performance at the very moment when all the Japanese in the world were shooting at him. Too often, the Mark 13 would hang up on its racks, and the joke was that the torpedo was so slow that the Japanese could write notes to each other to warn that it was coming. Some improvements were made in the Mark 13-1A torpedo, but this weapon was never completely satisfactory.

Even the termination of production of the sturdy Avenger on VJ-Day did not bring an end to the career of this little-recognized but rather important aircraft. In post-war US Navy service at a time when the enormous size of the Russian underwater fleet was a source of concern, Avengers were essential to ASW (anti-submarine warfare) operations until aircraft tailored for this mission could be developed. A variety of other tasks were taken on by the Avenger, including the first use of airborne warning and control, and Avengers served with friendly Allies – even the Japanese, from the establishment of their post-war armed forces on 1 July 1954 – until the early 1960s. From 1950 to 1957, 125 Avengers served in three Royal Canadian Navy squadrons.

Fat enough to be called the 'Turkey' the Avenger was also sturdy enough to take battle damage and come home. The Grumman TBF (TBM) Avenger survived the war to play a major role in the post-war US Navy. On 15 March 1950 these Avengers are on an anti-submarine warfare mission, flying over the destroyer USS John A. Bole (DD-755). (USN)

Squadrons which operated the Avenger included torpedo units VT-4, VT-7, VT-8, VT-10, VT-18, VT-20, VT-34, VT-40, VT-45, VT-51, VT-80, VT-83 and VT-88 (among many others). VT(N)-90 was designated as a night torpedo squadron. Composite squadrons (which performed anti-submarine work) included VC-9, VC-17, VC-30, VC-42, VC-55, VC-58, VC-65, VC-68, VC-71, VC-76, VC-88 and VC-94. Marine Corps units such as VMTB-132 and VMTB-234 flew Avengers from the decks of escort carriers.

Britain's Avenger units included the Royal Navy's Nos 820, 832, 849, 854, 855 and 857 Squadrons. Total British deliveries of the Tarpon/Avenger reached 958. Interestingly, two British Avengers were shooting down Nazi V-1 buzz bombs in 1944.

About a dozen Avengers remain in preserved and flyable status in the United States, including two TBF-1 aeroplanes and a larger number of TBM-3s. One example is TBF-1 number 2092 belonging to the Yankee Air Corps in Chino, California. Howard Pardue's Breckenridge Aviation Museum in Texas is the proud owner of TBM-3 Avenger bureau number 53522, now registered as N88HP, which appears regularly at air shows.

## Unsuccessful Sea Wolf

Almost forgotten in the roster of World War II bombers is the torpedo-bomber which failed to make the grade, the Consolidated TBY-2 Sea Wolf. If the obscure Sea Wolf is of interest, the reason is that it took the unheard-of route of being transferred from one manufacturing company to another.

This torpedo-bomber began life as the Vought XTBU-1. The US Navy wanted it. Vought lacked the facilities to build it. So the aircraft was turned over to Consolidated as the TBY-2 and an order for 1,100 was placed in September 1943. (No aircraft designated TBY-1 was built.) Only about 180 TBY-2s were actually built. On VJ-Day two squadrons of TBY-2s were getting ready to go into action. The end of hostilities ended any prospect of their being used in combat.

The three-man Sea Wolf had a maximum speed of 311mph (501km/h). It was a well-made aircraft and apparently handled well. Some sources say that it would have been marginally superior to the Grumman TBF Avenger. If so, the difference was not important for the Navy went with the Avenger and the latter aircraft achieved a significant place in history.

# B-29 Superfortress

L ong after the world boiled over and its people were thrown into the suffering and horror of the worst conflict in history, there remained more than a few sceptics who wondered if bombers were ever going to be much use. Long after Fortress and Liberator formations took command of the skies in Europe and began to extract a heavy toil from the Third Reich, there remained a smaller number of sceptics who thought this was an *ad hoc* situation. This airpower business was some kind of temporary fluke. Wars would still be decided on the ground. Japan would have to be invaded.

When the Boeing B-29 Superfortress became a reality and pressed the war against Japan, long-range airpower finally attained the kind of capability its supporters had been advocating for years.

In the end, the B-29 made it unnecessary to unleash Operation 'Olympic-Coronet', the invasion of the Japanese home islands scheduled for early 1946. 'Olympic-Coronet' would have involved amphibious landings in Kyushu and Tokyo Bay; the resulting armed struggle on the ground in Japan would have cost – said the official estimate – some 500,000 lives. Experts like Major Alexander Seversky had been saying for years that if long-range bombing were used properly, there would be no need for an invasion by ground troops. Indeed, had a long-range bomber been available earlier, much of the costly Pacific 'island-hopping' campaign by soldiers and Marines might have been averted. Like nothing before her, the B-29 was a 'super bomber' and a fitting means of bringing the world's worst war to an end.

Impetus behind the notion of a 'very heavy' bomber was another of the many forward-thinking airmen of the pre-war era, Major General Oscar Westover, Chief of the Air Corps, who died in a 21 September 1938 crash in Burbank, California. Westover and Air Corps engineering chief General Oliver Echols wanted a new super-bomber with even greater range than the B-17, which was then being subjected to rigorous scrutiny by Congress. Echols, who gave Boeing officials Claire Egtvedt and Ed Wells a tour of Wright Field, also gave them a pep talk about how a bomber could be developed with a range of 5,000 miles. The new aircraft would need flush rivets, low-drag gun turrets, skin-tight engine nacelles.

When Westover and Echols began tooting the long-range bomber horn in 1938, there was no money, Congress was not in a mood to appropriate any, and the nation was on a solidly isolationist course. Within a year or so, things changed. Major General Henry H. (Hap) Arnold, sworn in to replace Westover as Air Corps chief on 29 September 1938, followed up a Westover proposal in 1939 and secured authority to issue contracts for a 'very heavy' long-range bomber.

Arnold's action led to a 29 January 1940 specification and request for data which drew responses from four manufacturers, Boeing, Consolidated, Douglas and Lockheed.

Although Boeing was already hard at work on its Model 299, soon to be designated B-17, the company had the means to entertain other projects. Under the direction of company president Philip G. Johnson, the company submitted its proposal for the Model 341, a bomber able to fly faster than 400mph (644km/h) with 2,000lb (907kg) of bombs.

This was only the latest of a half-dozen Boeing designs for large bombers and in time it became the company's Model 345, powered by four of the newly developed 2,100hp Wright R-3350 Cyclone

Everything about the Boeing B-29 was superlative – it was the biggest US bomber, carried the most bombs, and flew furthest – and so it must have seemed to the Japanese Empire. Wichita-built B-29BW 44-69658 on an early test flight communicates its size to the camera. (Boeing)

Fresh from the factory, Boeing B-29 Superfortress 42-24612 plies through typical cloudy skies in the Pacific north-west. (USAF)

18-cylinder twin-row radial engines with General Electric B-11 turbo-superchargers for improved high-altitude performance.

The Wright engines proved trouble-prone: they overheated, chewed up valves, dripped oil, and could cause engine fires. As will be seen, engine fires were a persistent problem in the development and operation of the B-29.

Still, the engines became inseparable from the successful design of the B-29. The R-3350-13 model was fitted on the XB-29, the R-3350-21 on the service-test YB-29, the R-3350-23 on the production B-29, and the R-3350-57 on the B-29A.

As the new design unfolded on Boeing drawing-boards, there were problems. How, for example, could Boeing meet the requirement to create the world's first pressurized bomber with huge bomb bay doors which would have to be opened in flight? (The solution was make the bomb bays unpressurized and connect the front and rear pressure cabins via a sealed tunnel.) How would the firm design and build a sleek, streamlined bomber without the high drag caused by structural folds, tucks, and rivets? (The answer was thousands of precision bolts which rendered the aircraft as smooth as glass, with no projections.) Design of the B-29 proceeded and Boeing had a mock-up of the internal tunnel arrangement completed in early 1940.

## Big Bomber

The wing of the new bomber was an engineering marvel in its own right. The enormous wing flaps of the B-29 were not just larger than the wings of many fighter planes, they were the largest ever fitted on any aircraft. They kept the bomber's landing speed to an acceptably low rate, yet provided the required lift. The resulting low-drag wing design was known as the '117' wing.

Another way of looking at the design of the B-29 and its wing is to be reminded that British experience in the early months of World War II revealed the need for better armament and leak-proof fuel tanks. Boeing engineers had to weigh the added 3,000lb (1,360kg) of leak-proofing against the 2,000lb (907kg) of fuel required by this addition to achieve the specified range. Similarly, 2,500lb (1,134kg) of added armament meant 1,600lb (725kg) additional fuel. By selecting an aerofoil that could sustain twice the weight per square foot that the B-17 wing could, these trade-offs were surmounted. Later General Curtis E. LeMay proclaimed, 'The wing made the airplane'.

The B-29 Superfortress was indeed big: it had a wing span of 141ft 3in (43.05m), length of 99ft (30.18m), height of 29ft 7in (9.02m) and wing area of no less than 1,736sq ft (161.27m²). Specifications

A latter-generation Superfortress, preserved in the 1980s and wearing Korean War markings of the 1950s. Boeing B-29 Superfortress 45-21800 'Fifi' belongs to the Confederate Air Force and is a flying memorial to the B-29 and its successes in two wars. (David F. Brown)

An unusual wartime comparison from above of two very different Boeing products, the B-17G Fortress (top) and B-29 Superfortress. Far from being a development of the B-17, the larger B-29 was in fact a wholly new design, work on which had begun while the B-17 was still in a relatively early stage of development. The B-29 arrived too late to fight in Europe but made all the difference in the Pacific theatre. (via Dave Ostrowski)

called for the B-29 to reach a maximum speed of 358mph (576km/h) at 25,000ft (7,620m). To bring the war home to the enemy's back yard, range was 3,250 miles (5,230km). The world's first successful pressurized bomber had a service ceiling of 31,850ft (9,710m).

For defence the B-29 was equipped with remote-control, power-operated turrets which were electro-mechanically operated by an analogue computer located beneath the floorboards in the fuselage. Although various armaments were experimented with, the standard defensive weaponry for the B-29 Super-fortress became two 0.50in (12.7mm)

machine-guns in each of four turrets and three 0.50in (12.7mm) guns plus one 20mm cannon in the tail-gunner's position.

In May 1940 the Air Corps selected Boeing and Lockheed as winners of the competition for a 'very heavy' bomber. Lockheed's entry, the XB-30 – a version of the Model 749 Constellation airliner then under development – was never built. In June 1940 both companies were awarded contracts for full-scale mock-ups and wind-tunnel tests. On 24 August 1940 the Air Corps selected the Boeing design and contracted for the development and construction of two (later three) prototypes at a cost of $3,615,095.

The contract to produce prototypes, given the designation B-29, was signed in September 1940.

A massive production and support programme for the B-29 had been decided upon even before the olive-drab XB-29 prototype (41-002) took to the air some nine months after Pearl Harbor, on 21 September 1942, with Boeing test pilot Edmund T. (Eddie) Allen at the controls. The three XB-29s were delivered with three-bladed 17ft (5.18m) diameter propellers, although the production bombers had four-bladed 16ft 7in (5.04m) Hamilton Standard propellers; the latter were fitted with constant-speed governors and hydraulic operation for pitch change and feathering.

The second XB-29 (41-003) made its maiden flight on 30 December 1942. The bomber was an exceed-ingly complex aircraft for its time, but early testing seems to have been relatively trouble-free. Sadly, 41-003 crashed on a test flight only two months later, on 18 February 1943, killing Eddie Allen and his crew of eleven, plus nineteen people on the ground. The aircraft had been on approach and had failed to reach the runway's end. An engine fire, the first of many which were to be endemic to the B-29, was blamed for the crash.

By the time the third XB-29 flew on 16 June 1943, the first service-test YB-29 following soon afterward, the 'very heavy' bomber programme was moving with enormous momentum.

Under the massive manufacturing programme launched in the wake of Pearl Harbor, major sub-assemblies for the B-29 were churned out in as many

Left: Boeing F-13 Superfortress 42-24583, the photo-reconnaissance version of the famous bomber, had special camera installations which included tri-metrogon K-22, K-18 or special flash-bulb night aerial cameras. Boeing F-13s did the major part of the high-altitude mapping of the Japanese home islands before the surrender. These aircraft were redesignated RB-29 after the war. (via Dave Ostrowski)

Right: On a typical B-29 Superfortress base in the Western Pacific, bombers were stretched out as far as the eye could see. Little concern was shown for protection from possible Japanese air attack, since the enemy's air arm no longer had this capability. On big missions, take-offs were made only moments apart and the first priority of any bomber crew which got into trouble was to get out of the way so that the crew behind could complete the take-off and press on with the mission. (via Dave Ostrowski)

Left: Boeing B-29 Superfortress 42-93844. (USAF)

as 60 different plants; the enormous engine nacelles, for example, each as big as a P-47, came from a new Cleveland facility operated by the Fisher Body Division of General Motors. Final assembly of the Superfortress was carried out at no fewer than four locations, Boeing at Renton, Washington, and Wichita, Kansas; Martin at Omaha, Nebraska; and Bell at Marietta, Georgia. More than $3,000 million had been invested in the B-29 construction programme before the first operational Superfortress appeared.

There can be no denying that the B-29 was a marvel of American industry, but the crash of the second prototype threw the programme in jeopardy. Only when General Arnold guaranteed that the programme would be closely monitored by military people did it continue – in the face of some opposition. Boeing's first Wichita-built Superfortress (42-6205) was delivered on 7 October 1943, the company's first Renton-produced B-29A (42-93824) on 1 January 1944. The first Bell-made Superfort from Marietta (42-63352) was accepted on 30 December 1943 and the first from Martin in Omaha (42-65202) came on 31 May 1944.

First trickling, then pouring from factory lines, designed and tested and produced in record time, the B-29 was not without its flaws, most of them attributable to the haste with which the aircraft was being rushed into the war. Early machines went to a processing centre in Salina, Kansas, where more than 9,900 faults in the first 175 airframes, earmarked for the newly formed 58th Bomb Wing, were set right by a 600-man task force in the 'Kansas Blitz'.

Post-war films tended to glorify the B-29, and it was certainly true that the bomber achieved greatness and became loved by many who flew her. But especially in the early days, the Superfortress seemed spooked. The aircraft was not well-loved in the beginning. Lt Col Bob Filson, a bombardier who went to Tinian and logged 548 combat hours, was one of many B-29 fliers who was superstitious. Every time he boarded his B-29, he always entered and exited the same way. 'I figured if I did it the same way every time, I'd be OK. I saw so many friends die . . .'

## Crew Composition

The bombardier, of course, was the 'point man' – up in that bulbous nose ahead of the other crew members. The difficult job he faced was described by Colonel Eugene L. Eubank, commander of the 19th Bomb Group. Of the bombardier, Eubank said, 'The greatest bombing planes in the world take him into battle through every opposition, and in 30 seconds over the target he must vindicate the greatest responsibility ever placed upon an individual soldier in the line of duty.'

The radar bombing-navigation aid which put the B-29 at the forefront of technology was the AN/APQ-13 system, created by the Massachusetts Institute of Technology and the Bell Telephone Labs. It used a 30in (0.76m) radar antenna located in a hemispherical radome installed between the two bomb bays. The downward-pointing radome was at times retouched out of photos released during the war, but it was standard equipment.

In all, five of the eleven men aboard a B-29 were officers: the aircraft commander (pilot), co-pilot, bombardier, navigator and flight engineer. The remaining six enlisted men were the radio-operator, radar-operator, central fire control gunner, left and right gunners, and the tail gunner. On some missions, additional crewmen performed extra functions, as the bomber had some room to carry extra people.

It has been a tradition in American bomber aviation to send an aircraft into battle with a 'hard' crew: the same men fly with each other, mission after mission. Pilot, co-pilot and flight engineer, in particular, must function as a finely honed team, each man understanding and predicting the other's needs and actions.

The aircraft commander sat in the left seat, handled the B-29, and led the crew. He was the most important member of the crew. Whether or not it produces good pilots, the American military system

B-29 in flight. (Boeing)

has always produced superb officers, and while an occasional aircraft commander may have lacked the fine touch at the controls, it was rare when he lacked leadership. Like all commanders, he might have to snap orders, especially in the heat of the battle – but first, he had to build up the crew's respect. Usually the aircraft commander of a B-29 succeeded in this most difficult task of leading men. On the rare occasion when he didn't, nothing else worked.

Incredibly, once this mighty bomber had been fielded and its crews trained, it remained unclear how the B-29 would be employed in the campaign against Japan. Some air generals started planning for the bombing of Japan from bases on the Asian mainland in Nationalist China.

For the purpose of ferrying larger numbers of B-29s eastwards across the Atlantic and Africa to the

Asian mainland, the US spent millions to develop the Roberts Field aerodrome near Monrovia, Liberia. In that West African backwater, building a state-of-the-art airfield turned out to be an act of unparalleled generosity on the part of the US Government, which picked up the tab but ended up not needing Roberts very much at all for B-29 operations. The airfield remains one of Africa's best today.

After several plans were developed, it was finally decided to deploy the 58th Bomb Wing to India and to advanced bases in China. Conditions in China were far from optimum for the B-29, but advanced teams were sent to establish an infra-structure to handle fuel, ordnance and maintenance needs.

In spite of their efforts, B-29s continued to experience engine fires and other difficulties when the 58th took the new bombers to the China-Burma-India Theatre. The fires remained a problem with the B-29 fleet even as late as VJ-Day. In March 1944 the first B-29 was flown to India by Colonel Leonard (Jake) Harman and turned over to the 20th Bomber Command led by General K. B. Wolfe. A veritable armada followed and the first two surmounting the 'Hump' arrived at Chengtu, China, on 24 April 1944.

On 26 April 1944 a B-29 tail gunner on a ferry flight over China shot down a Nakajima Ki.43 (Oscar) fighter, drawing first blood for the Superfortress. On 5 June 1944 the B-29 made its first actual combat mission, some 98 aircraft proceeding to Bangkok to bomb marshalling yards. On 14 June 1944 the 20th Bomber Command sent 75 B-29s to strike the iron and steel works at Yawata in western Japan. In those early days mechanical and other problems contributed to the loss of several aircraft,

even as the campaign from bases in China grew more intense.

But in the recently completed Pentagon building in Washington, some were arguing that the aerial campaign against the Japanese homeland might best be mounted from the Marianas. This Pacific island group, which included Saipan, Tinian and Guam (the lat-named being US territory), lay just 1,800 miles (2,896km) from key industrial and military targets on the main Japanese island of Honshu. As the 'island-hopping' campaign seized these specks on the ocean, US naval construction battalions moved into Tinian, and there, created the largest bomber base ever built – with four parallel runways, each 2 miles (3.2km) long – which in time handled up to 200 B-29s operated by the 313th Bomb Wing and the 509th Composite Group.

Among those who favoured assaulting Japan from the Marianas Islands was General Haywood S. ('Possum') Hansell, an experienced 'bomber general' from the fighting in Europe who had successfully made the transition from B-17 to B-29. Hansell arrived in the Western Pacific aboard a B-29 nicknamed 'Joltin' Josie', took charge of 21st Bomber

Command, and organized the aerial campaign against Japan. In due course he was replaced by General Curtis LeMay.

LeMay concluded that high-altitude precision bombing was not effective and decided to deliver a destructive blow with incendiary bombs. The idea was not wholly LeMay's: the Army had constructed a mock-up Japanese city at its Dugway, Utah, proving ground and had discovered that the wood-and-paper construction of Japan's buildings lent itself to destruction using fire-bombs. The change also seemed to be borne out by the results of the first incendiary strikes against Japanese targets on 25 February 1945 and 4 March 1945, but LeMay decided to go a step further. He stripped his B-29s of most of their guns to reduce weight and launched a devastating mission against Tokyo on the night of 9/10 March 1945 with his bombers flying down at a scant 6,000ft.

The results were like something out of hell. The incendiaries caused the hottest fires that have ever burned on this planet, and destruction greater than that of both subsequent atomic bombs put together. High winds fanned the flames into an inferno.

Nose sections of four-engined Boeing B-29 Superfortress bombers being assembled by 'Rosie the Riveter'-style factory workers at the Boeing Aircraft Company, Renton, Washington. Visible is the opening on the top of the aircraft fuselage intended for a power-operated gun turret. (Boeing)

Two views of the enormous industrial power which 'whipped' Japan. No other nation possessed the riches, the resources, the sheer manufacturing potential to build so many aircraft, so fast. Times have changed, but in the 1940s Americans could build B-29 Superfortress bombers like this secure in the knowledge that no one else could match their productivity. (Boeing)

Bombers still coming in to drop their loads were buffeted by rising hot air and some crashed. The blaze consumed some 16 square miles of the capital, killed 83,000 people, injured 40,000, and left half the population of Tokyo homeless. It was a terrible way to wage war, but for Americans it was more merciful than an amphibious invasion of Japan.

The surrender of Germany in May 1945 did not end fighting in the Pacific, however. Nor did Japan seem inclined to surrender, even though B-29s now ruled the skies over the Japanese home islands.

## New Bomb

In remote New Mexico mountains at Los Alamos, scientists under J. Robert Oppenheimer had been working in secret to develop a new bomb based on the long-understood theory that critical atomic masses could combine to produce an enormous explosion. Before any such bomb existed, Colonel Paul Tibbets was sent to equally remote Wendover airfield, Utah, to form the B-29-equipped 509th Composite Group. Members of the 509th were hand-picked, not only pilots but every crew member, and were told only that they were embarked on a mission of very great importance. Except for Tibbets, none knew their real mission as they arrived in the Utah desert to begin flying their new aircraft under new conditions.

Today Wendover is a small city in a glass-like flat desert far removed from America's festering set of urban problems. In 1944, when Tibbets took his B-29s to Wendover, the city of Wendover was – nothing. One crewman remembers a solitary petrol station and a general store, both useless since the B-29 fliers were forbidden from leaving the base anyway. Wendover was flat, remote, bleak, hot: the mule teams that plied the desert fell beneath the shadows of massive four-engined bombers, about which nobody was saying much. The bombers were there. Even the men who flew them didn't now what they were doing.

Why, for example, were the bomber crews ordered to practise abrupt, gut-wrenching turns which would put the massive B-29 into a violent dive just after releasing the bomb load? It was as if the bomb load could somehow harm the B-29 after leaving the bomb bay, but that was impossible, wasn't it? Or was there some kind of secret bomb under development? One pilot visualized a 5,000lb (2,270kg), box-finned bomb so powerful that it could obliterate an entire city block. Could there be a bomb so big? And even so, why the urgency in getting the B-29 out of harm's way once it was dropped?

In scientific circles, more than a few physicists were aware that atoms could be split and that speculation existed about a future bomb far larger

Pipe-smoking Colonel Paul V. Tibbets and the crew of his Boeing B-29 Superfortress (44-86292), an aircraft which had actually been assigned to another pilot until Tibbets took it over for the Hiroshima mission. The Superfortress is now part of the collection belonging to the Smithsonian Institution's National Air and Space Museum. (USAF)

than any blockbuster. Many people knew even more. When Truman finally told Stalin that the US was developing a new bomb of unspeakable power, Stalin already knew: his agents had penetrated both Los Alamos and Wendover. Apart from the public, press and Congress, the crews of Paul Tibbets' B-29s may have been among the few who didn't know, didn't even suspect, the enormity of what they were getting into.

Oppenheimer and General Leslie Groves, head of the 'Manhattan' project, as it was known, took a walk out in the desert 200 miles (320km) south of Los Alamos and chose the Trinity Site, not far from where Oppenheimer had ridden horses in earlier years, to test their brainchild. At one time they were going to test the first atomic bomb inside a railroad car-sized iron container, called 'Jumbo', so that if the weapon failed to detonate its critical materials could be saved. 'Jumbo' weighed hundreds of tons and was carted all over New Mexico, but in the end the world's first atomic bomb was set off without being enclosed in a container. Oppenheimer's words, from the literature of India, are etched in the consciousness forever to describe that first bomb exploding in the American desert: 'I am become death, destroyer of worlds.'

By the time Tibbets' 509th Bomb Group was ready to leave Wendover for the enormous airfield on the Pacific island of Tinian – at that time, the most populous and busiest airfield in the world – that first atomic device was exploded at New Mexico's Trinity Site in July 1945. The 509th arrived at Tinian and was summarily shunted to a corner of the base and largely (but not entirely) isolated. B-29 Superfortress crews in other bomb groups jostled and razzed these men, who kept practising unusual flying tactics, but never seemed to go out and bomb Japan. All the other B-29 outfits were flying over Hirohito's homeland daily, at some risk, and were inflicting crippling damage on Japan's ability to wage war. It has been argued, and is almost certainly true, that the B-29 Superfortress would have defeated Japan in about the same duration of time even if Tibbets' men had never done anything but practice.

This is an important point about B-29 operations against the Japanese Empire and one which bears repeating. Even if there had been no atomic bomb, the sustained B-29 campaign was levelling Japan. Men like 'Possum' Hansell and Curtis LeMay were behind the greatest unleashing of aerial destruction yet.

On 6 August 1945 Tibbets exercised rank over another pilot to make himself pilot of the other flier's B-29, which Tibbets named 'Enola Gay' after his mother. The 509th skipper flew the mission which dropped the first atomic bomb on Hiroshima. Actual fusing and preparation of the bomb was carried out by Navy Captain Deke Parsons, a crewmember.

The mushroom cloud billowing 20,000ft (6,096m) above the medium-sized Japanese city of Hiroshima on 6 August 1945. These views were probably taken from Major Claude Eatherly's B-29 Superfortress which flew a reconnaissance mission on the heels of Colonel Paul Tibbets' B-29. In post-war years, Eatherly suffered personal difficulties while convincing others that he was, in fact, *The Hiroshima Pilot*, the title of William Bradford Huie's book about him. (USAF)

A blinding flash of light, a wall of heat, and a billowing mushroom cloud appeared over the horror that had been Hiroshima, where 78,000 people died and 51,000 were injured.

The carnage was repeated on 9 August 1945 when Major Charles Sweeney, commanding a B-29 named 'Bock's Car', diverted from his primary target at Kokura and dropped an atomic bomb on Nagasaki. Because that city lay inside ridgelines which run perpendicular to the sea, the number of immediate deaths was kept to 35,000 – as if numbers of such a magnitude can be grasped.

The author has visited both Hiroshima and Nagasaki: they are testimony to the cruelty of war.

The Boeing B-29 Superfortress had won the war against Japan – perhaps even before either atomic bomb fell. After the two bombs, Japan surrendered on 15 August 1945. The Allies had held out for unconditional surrender and got it.

## B-29 Units

Although used in combat only in the Pacific and China theatres, having arrived in service too late to be employed effectively against Germany, the B-29 Superfortress belonged, at one time or another, to a remarkable number of USAAF bomb groups, beginning (in the combat theatre) with the 462nd Bomb Group which flew the first Superfortress mission to Japan on 15 June 1944. In the slow easy days before the war, it was not unusual for a solitary bomb group to be the only tenant at an Army air base: at one point in 1945 there were eleven bomb groups stationed on Tinian!

North Field at Guam in April 1945 was only marginally smaller, B-29s being stretched out everywhere as far as the eye could see, with a deceptively tranquil background of what remained of the palm trees in the area. When Iwo Jima was taken – in one of the bloodiest battles of all time, costing 5,000 Marine casualties in the first few hours – an airfield grew among volcanic outcroppings and damaged aircraft had a runway they could reach while limping away from Japan.

It was at about this time that the 'wing' replaced the 'group' as the principal USAAF unit. The 73rd Wing moved with its B-29s to Saipan in late 1944 and at that time had a number of subordinate groups such as the 499th. In theory, a wing consists of groups which, in turn, consist of squadrons. However, as the wing became the standard major formation, the group eventually disappeared as a distinct unit in Air Force lineage, with the wing commander being directly in charge of his squadron commanders.

Customs, habits, and individual aircraft markings varied enormously among the groups using the Superfortress. For example, during a period when colourful markings were being frowned upon, the commander of the 462nd Bomb Group personally approached General LeMay and secured permission to retain red rudders on his B-29s.

Missions varied too. Most B-29 crews simply dropped bombs on Japan, and did their best to complete this odious task without being killed by fighters or anti-aircraft fire. But the 313th Bomb Group drew the job of laying aerial mines along the Korean coast. Some B-29 crews were assigned the

Atomic bomb of the 'Little Boy' type, dropped by Colonel Paul Tibbets' B-29 Superfortress 'Enola Gay' on Hiroshima, 6 August 1945. The bomb weighed a 9,000lb (4,082kg) and when detonated had an explosive yield of 20,000 tons (18 million kilogrammes) of high explosive. The B-29 Superfortresses of the 509th Bomb Group on Tinian were specially equipped to carry the atomic bomb. (USAF)

unglamorous duty of hauling fuel, their bombers becoming tankers. Several squadrons operated F-13A Superfortresses on photoreconnaissance missions.

B-29 wings were the 73rd, 313th, and 314th. USAAF Bomb Groups which operated the Superfortress included the 6th, 9th, 19th, 29th, 39th, 40th, 58th, 313th, 314th, 315th, 331st, 444th, 462nd, 468th, 497th, 498th, 499th, 500th, 505th and 509th. Among photo squadrons equipped with F-13A Superfortresses were the 1st and 13th.

## B-29 Versions

While the war in the Pacific was under way, other versions of the B-29 came into service. 117 aircraft were converted for photo-reconnaissance duties under the designation F-13A. As has been noted earlier, the XB-39 was an experimental conversion of a service-test YB-29 fitted with four Allison V-3420 double liquid-cooled engines, while the XB-44 was a similar conversion of a basic B-29 airframe with 3,000hp R-4360-33 Wasp Major engines, and was subsequently redesignated B-29D.

Post-war variants included the SB-29 search-and-rescue and WB-29 weather-reconnaissance Superfortresses. When Strategic Air Command was founded in May 1946, an early priority was to establish effective air-to-air refuelling on long-range combat missions, and the Superfortress became the first widely employed tanker. The first tankers were converted by Boeing in 1948 to become KB-29Ms, using hose and reel systems. The KB-29P tanker introduced the flying boom method of aerial refuelling, still in use today, wherein a telescoping metal

pipe passes fuel to the receiver aircraft under pressure. YKB-29J and KB-29T Superfortress tanker variants were also built.

A number of other B-29 versions came during the post-war years, some as airborne 'mother ships' for jet and rocket-propelled research aircraft. The Navy acquired some aircraft for mother ship duties as the PB2B-1. At least a few Superforts were used to tow targets. A number of TB-29 Superfortresses were used for training and radar calibration duties. RB-29 reconnaissance aircraft prowled the frontiers of the Soviet Union. The post-war B-50 bomber was based on the B-29 design.

As an interim step until British jet bombers could be developed and placed into service, an agreement signed on 27 January 1950 made B-29s available to the Royal Air Force. On 20 March 1950 the first Superfortresses were handed over to the RAF in a ceremony at Andrews AFB, Maryland, and the new British operators immediately decided to name the aeroplane the Washington – certainly the first time an armed force named an aircraft after a general of a victorious enemy. The Washington bombers (88 had been delivered) were eventually returned to the US in 1953–54, but not until they had spent a considerable time adding to Britain's strategic deterrent.

The B-29 Superfortress remained in widespread service within the newly independent United States Air Force when a new war erupted in Korea on 25 June 1950. The combat saga of the B-29 continued, the Korean portion being outside the scope of this work. Using a captured B-29 which landed on their territory during the fighting against Japan, the

'Bock's Car', subtitled 'Salt Lake [to] Nagasaki', is Boeing B-29-36-MO Superfortress 44-27297, manufactured under licence by Martin in Omaha. Piloting this aircraft, Major Charles Sweeney dropped the second atomic bomb of the war, not on his prime target of Kokura which was hidden beneath cloud cover, but on the port of Nagasaki. (USAF)

Soviets copied the B-29 design almost rivet for rivet, producing the externally identical Tupolev Tu-4.

Today the aviation buff can still get a first-hand look at the mighty four-engined bomber which played such a vital role in our recent history. In the 1950s small children, including this author, could crawl around inside Colonel Paul Tibbets' 'Enola Gay' (44-86292), finding birds' nests inside the tunnel over the bomb bay. The Hiroshima bomber was then parked in an accessible area of Andrews Air Force Base, Maryland, and is now among the holdings of the Smithsonian Institution's National Air and Space Museum, although not yet on permanent display.

Perhaps even better known, and certainly more visible since it remains in flying condition, is 'Fifi', a former TB-29A operated by the Confederate Air Force and incidentally the aircraft used to play 'Enola Gay' in a television film.

## Big Bombers

Victory, the end of global conflict, 15 August 1945, had to be a mixed and bittersweet moment for many, not least the families of the many men who gave their lives in all the bombers that failed to complete the war. There may have been something symbolic about the first post-hostilities flight over Japan by a brace of Superfortresses which went in at low level, bombed and shot no one, and came away with crews remarking upon the beauty and serenity of the nation they had transformed into an industrial wasteland. During the 1950–53 Korean conflict, it was said that although Japanese farmers working near US air bases always looked up when any other aircraft took off or landed, they never raised their heads to look at the B-29, the reason never being fully explained. While the war was still going on, there was a rather elaborate display of the wreckage of a B-29 in a Japanese city, complete with a colourful cutaway drawing mounted beside the actual aircraft; an American post-war plan to display a B-29 at a public event was cancelled without explanation by the US top brass.

It is difficult to comprehend how much progress was made in the design, development and operational and combat use of bombers during the period of American involvement (1941–45) in that great conflict. Before Pearl Harbor, the long-range bomber was little more than an idea in the minds of a few visionaries. After VJ-Day, the B-29 Superfortress and the country which had built it enjoyed unchallenged dominance of every inch of the planet. We had gone from fabric control surfaces to the first jet-powered aircraft, from two engines to four and soon thereafter six, then ten. We had gone from a combat radius of

Typical of post-war Superfortresses is this KB-29M tanker of the 55th Air Refueling Squadron from Forbes AFB in Topeka, Kansas. The KB-29M tanker used the British 'hose and drogue' method of refuelling receiver aircraft. (via Robert F. Dorr)

less than a hundred miles to over a thousand. We had progressed from being able to blow a hole in a swamp to being able to obliterate the earth itself.

The machines of war, the aircraft which carried men through bullet-riddled skies, have been the subject of this volume. In a larger sense, of course, it makes little real difference whether history records what happened to the B-26G or the liquid-cooled Superfortresses or the container for an atomic bomb that wasn't used. After all, if events had not transpired the way they did, events would have unfolded in some other fashion. Men would still have found ways to unleash the terrible destructive power of industrial warfare on each other, bombers would still have rained death from the heavens, and people would still have died.

What does matter, and what we tend to forget so easily – especially among the younger generation who are most likely to find something new in this book – what matters above all else is that free men were willing to employ force of arms in the defence of liberty. In today's world we tend, too easily, to adopt the callous view that there exists no clear difference between good and evil, between freedom and tyranny, between complacency and courage. In the 1980s we forget that good men who valued freedom also possessed the courage to fight for it. To our everlasting damnation, a few of us in the

world of the aviation enthusiast still break bread and share drink with those who fought for the Third Reich, out of some misguided sense that we were all brothers in arms. We were not. Good men who valued freedom and possessed courage went forth in the American bombers of World War II and helped us to survive.

Yes, we lost twelve thousand bombers. Yes, we lost countless thousands of men. It is a disservice to those men – a slap in the face – to invite some Luftwaffe pilot to next week's gathering of warbird enthusiasts, to pretend that all is forgiven, to overlook the reprehensible horrors for which the Luftwaffe fought. But it would be a greater disservice to forget that the world truly is divided, to forget that tyrants remain, to forget that the issues for which those bomber crews fought were and are absolutely without ambiguity, absolutely clearcut.

From the Boeing XB-15 to the mighty B-29 Superfortress, from Dauntlesses at Midway to incendiaries over Tokyo, the American bombers of World War II fought and won a struggle that was necessary and just. The sad truth is that freedom does not survive for long without challenge, and courage must be tested every generation. The sadder truth is that we need to look very hard at ourselves as the twentieth century draws to an end and to ask ourselves whether we could do it again if we had to.

Evidence of the success of the relentless B-29 Superfortress campaign against the Japanese homeland. Two weeks after the Emperor's 15 August 1945 statement of surrender, the formal document ending hostilities is signed – by Namoro Shigomitsu for the Emperor and by Admiral of the Fleet Chester Nimitz for the Allies. Had the four-engined Boeing bomber not been available to raze Japan's war-making installations, the cessation of hostilities might have been delayed for months or years. (USN)

# Index

Quality Printing By:
Bath Press Ltd.
Lower Bristol Road
Bath
Avon BA2 3BL
England